A Touchstone Book

VIET ROCK

∎

COMINGS AND GOINGS

∎

KEEP TIGHTLY CLOSED
IN A COOL DRY PLACE

∎

THE GLOAMING,
OH MY DARLING

∎

four plays by
MEGAN TERRY

with an introduction by
RICHARD SCHECHNER

A Touchstone Book
Published by
SIMON AND SCHUSTER

CONTENTS

■

INTRODUCTION

◼

The Playwright as Wrighter

Megan Terry doesn't write plays, she wrights them. This cunning homonym indicates a return of the playwright to his original profession. Until the Renaissance, and sporadically since then, the making of plays was not the work of writers (who were poets and had their own profession) but of those who were part of the theatre. Some—Molière, Shakespeare—were actors; others—Brecht, Aeschylus—were directors. All understood that the basic mode of theatre was performance. Few plays were distributed as literary texts in their own time. Even Shakespeare had to wait until he was in his grave seven years before the First Folio appeared. Plays were for playing, and books for reading.

The Renaissance, with its love of documents, changed all that. History was rediscovered and we exist amid the cherished residues of dozens of cultures; no longer can we get through the day without some recourse to the library or museum (at home or institutionalized), some awesome confrontation with a "masterpiece." It's a bit frightening, all that accumulating greatness, and more so in the performing arts than in the others. For the repertory asks to be played and the high-water marks are indeed high. However, recently we have reached a turning point; Renaissance rules and assumptions are no longer that important. Theatre and literature have diverged once again. One need not be a scholar of Antonin Artaud or

Bertolt Brecht to recognize that performance, action, and event are the key terms of our theatre—and that these terms are not literary. Surely rhetoric has its place in the theatre, but only as one more differentiated form of action. Megan Terry is one playwright among several who know that action is the soul of drama.

Gordon Craig—madman, genius, failure—suggested that Shakespeare wrote by lifting story-segments from English history chronicles or Italian novellas (and elsewhere) and asking his actors to improvise these scenes. A scribe wrote down what the actors said and Shakespeare went home to rework these crude lines into the iambics of his great plays. The actors gave him what no man working alone could get: a living sense of interaction, irony in depth, different linguistic and gestural patterns, simultaneity. Craig's suggestion has logical, if not historical, merit. Shakespeare's plays are unique for their "thickness," the complicated interweave of character, motive, and scene. They work on many levels at once and appeal to a multi-class audience. Their fluidity and busyness is drawn from the streets and an imagination as flexible as electronic circuitry. Shakespeare's plays are free from subjectivity; as Keats noted, the playwright had a "negative capability," an ability to stay out of his plays. If we are to believe Craig, Shakespeare stayed out because he was never in; he assembled, reworked, manipulated, phrased, arranged. But the first lines of the action were shown to him by his actors. Shakespeare's universal imagination is that of the metamorphosizing collagist, the great transformer. His gifts and tools included theft. For his unadorned poetry, see the *Sonnets*.

Surely Megan Terry is not Shakespeare—there are thieves and thieves. But her methods are like those Craig attributed to Shakespeare and her *Viet Rock* is Elizabethan in scope and tone. There we see a war unfold, from birth to death, from death back to life; we see both sides, more than two sides; there is irony, parody, seriousness; there are dramatic scenes and music, patter scenes, monologue, pantomime. A grab bag as impertinent as anything the Elizabethans concocted; a conglomeration of styles, sources, and effects. Yet the play has a unity. Why, and where is it?

One seeks Miss Terry not first in her plays nor in herself, but in the Open Theatre—that expanding and contracting group, directed by Joseph Chaikin (but not dominated by him), which is laying the groundwork for the American theatre's future. Not the Open Theatre alone, of course: but a way of thinking most clearly exemplified by the Open Theatre, present also in Second City-with-Paul Sills, the Living Theatre, and some other stirrings off Broadway and around the country. Founded in September 1963, the Open Theatre's goals, as defined by Chaikin, are "to redefine the limits of the stage experience, or unfix them. To find ways of reaching each other and the audience." Playwrights are an important part of the Open Theatre. They "suggest forms for us—later these are often written out. These pieces are inspired by the actors' work. You see, there's a give-and-take. After the writer has suggested a form—I don't like 'plot' because these things are often much simpler than a plot—we begin to improvise with them. We select what language to use. Very often this is a 'language' of our own, sounds which communicate. . . . The mode of the language depends on the form of the improvisation, its goals, and our own warm-up. . . . We're in no hurry." Miss Terry runs a playwright's workshop for the Open Theatre, and *Viet Rock* was developed in that workshop. *Keep Tightly Closed* began as an actors' project for the Open Theatre; *Comings and Goings* is, in Miss Terry's words, "an enjoyment of technique, pure virtuosity on the part of the actors."

These are hints leading us to a method of working that is significantly different from what playwrights have been accustomed to. Miss Terry's plays are made with her actors. They begin as "notions," move through a chrysalis stage of improvisation, become "solidified" in a text, and are produced. But this solidification is not final; the plays themselves, like the performances, evolve. Sometimes, in my opinion at least, they over-evolve—they achieve a balance and then lose it again. I enjoyed the "first" version of *Viet Rock* at the Café La Mama Experimental Theatre Club in New York more than I did its "revised" version at Yale University. But the idea of constant revision is exciting; it puts the playwright on the same ground as the actors, and in the same peril of over-performing. Of course, once the texts have been printed—as in this book—the plays become "literature," like it or not. But Miss Terry's plays in print do not have the same authority as, say, the texts of Arthur Miller; and this lack of authority is to the plays' advantage. The texts, as Gide would say, remain "pretexts" for productions; their staging should not be a re-creation so much as a reconstruction.

If the basic mood of the Open Theatre is participation, its essential exercise is the "transformation." According to Peter Feldman who directed the Open Theatre production of *Keep Tightly Closed,* "The transformation is adapted from a Second City Workshop device. . . . It is an improvisation in which the established realities or 'given circumstances' (the Method phrase) of the scene change several times during the course of the action. What may change are character and/or situation and/or time and/or objectives. Whatever realities are established at the beginning are destroyed after a few minutes and replaced by others. Then these are in turn destroyed and replaced. These changes occur swiftly and *almost without transition,* until the audience's dependence upon any fixed reality is called into question."

In other words, a transformation is a realistic acting exercise infused with the tensions and strategies of a game. The actor is no longer "playing his reality," but rather "playing with a set of quick-changing realities." The inner rules of realistic acting are surrounded by an outer set of rules which determine

10

the rate and kind of change. Each unit within a set of transformations is (or can be) as "real" as any bit of naturalistic
acting; but the quick changes from one bit to another give the
over-all effect of kaleidoscope, fluidity, and scenic explosion.
Like many important new techniques, the transformation is
simple; it does not make unusual demands on the actor. It
merely asks him to give up his conventional, play-long identification with a role. The actor no longer plays out a continuity but a set of interrelated (and sometimes unrelated)
actions, each of which is self-contained. He gets from one
action to the next not by establishing for himself a logical,
motivational connective but by following the "rules of the
game" which say that at a certain time, on a certain cue, action
A ends and action B begins. It is no more difficult for the
actor to make these adjustments then it is for a football player
to run with the ball on one play and block for the ball carrier
on the next. Transformations do not change acting but the
rules governing the use of acting.

In changing these rules, however, new situations are possible for performance and through that for playwrights. If the
actor no longer has to make naturalistic connectives between
scenes, the playwright, too, can jump from situation to situation structuring his play on the progression of action-blocs
rather than on motivationally connected sequences, each of
which is psychologically contained in a larger unit—beat,
scene, act, play. The new action-blocs (such as Miss Terry
uses in her plays) can relate to each other in pre-logical ways.
They can compress, go off on tangents, serve as counterpoint,
stop plot development to explore mood, and so on. The device is not expressionistic because it makes no attempt to
"represent the mind" of the playwright or the character. Perhaps a few examples from Miss Terry's plays will make the
value of transformations clearer.

Act One of *Viet Rock* ends with a Senate Hearing investigating differing attitudes toward the Vietnamese war. Two

Senators are running the hearing and a variety of witnesses have been called to testify, among them figures which seem to represent Eleanor Roosevelt, Cassius Clay, General LeMay, the Madonna, and Jesus Christ. After each witness testifies (and several times in the midst of the testimony), the actors playing the roles switch parts. The Madonna becomes a Senator, Clay becomes Jesus, and so on. There is no "reason" for these switches; that is, neither Miss Terry nor the director wished to tell us that the Madonna equals Senator. What happens is that the audience's usual habit of identifying actor and character is challenged and broken. One watches the action (hilarious, serious parody) and not the actors. And the action of the scene becomes much clearer because of the breakdown in the actor-character relationship. The American way of "investigation," and the American "consensus," is put to a test. Neither right nor left is spared. And the great "mainstream," which finally carries the scene in triumph, is the most brutally and ironically satirized. Because each actor brings to each bit his own set of gestures and reading of lines, the underlying pattern of the scene emerges more sharply, unmitigated by this or that powerful (or weak) interpretation. One also has the sense, struck home by comparatively few actors, of a national phenomenon: a crowded room, a great variety of senators and witnesses and observers. All this is achieved with great theatrical economy, without slides, movies, or complicated sets.

In *Keep Tightly Closed* both character and situation change. At one moment there are three men in a cell, linked by murder. Jaspers hired Michaels to hire Gregory to kill Jaspers' wife. Gregory botched the job and all three are serving out life sentences. Shades of the Sheppard murder case, *Deathwatch,* and *No Exit*. Jaspers wants to force Gregory into signing a confession that would exonerate Michaels and Jaspers. The tortures which Jaspers and Michaels put Gregory through are represented by a series of transformations. Gregory be-

12

comes an Indian Chief captured by two of General Custer's soldiers. He is dismembered. Later Gregory becomes Captain John Smith bringing water to two dying members of Smith's expedition in Virginia. The three of them re-enact the murder, with Jaspers playing his own wife. Gregory and Michaels play Jaspers' two young children consoling their father after the murder. And so on. Between these sharp, often satirical scenes the relationship in the cell develops. The three men are locked together; they will not be sprung. The transformations serve several purposes. They explode a routine situation into a set of exciting theatrical images; they reinforce, expand, and explore the varieties of relationships among the three men; they make concrete the fantasies of the prisoners. But these fantasies are shown in a non-psychological way: there is no hint that the transformations are what the characters are thinking. At best, they are what the characters might be thinking were they equipped to think in theatrical terms. As such, the transformations are not naturalistic or expressionistic devices, but active models of the larger situation.

In modern drama we are accustomed to the formula: actor equals character equals life. The audience sees the play and identifies with the characters and the story they enact; a "symbolic reality" is created which metaphorically recapitulates a life-experience. The actor studies his role and seeks means of relating his own psychic and physical gestures to those of the character. In terms popular among today's actors, he seeks a "through line of action" expressed in a set of interrelated and organically developing "objectives," each of which is situated within the "given circumstances" of the play. Thus the audience on one side and the actors on the other try to extend the character into life. Play scripts encourage this task because most plays are recapitulations of possible life-experiences. The modern tendency of valuing individuality as an ideal reinforces this kind of interpretation of theatrical texts. Everything from the "beat" within a scene to the entire play

13

is tied into an organic life-form held together by the inter-relation between character and action. The form of a play thus conceived and acted is one of contained and containing boxes in which the "lives" of the characters are axes. Thus there is a harmonious consistency between the parts of the play and between these parts and the play's characters. Characters develop, change strategies, succeed, and fail—all within the context of the "given circumstances" of beat, scene, act, and play.

Transformations introduce an entirely different kind of construction, one with exciting possibilities for the playwright (as Miss Terry knows). The play is no longer a consistent set of interrelated units. It may or may not have an over-all harmony in its construction. *Viet Rock, Keep Tightly Closed,* and *In the Gloaming* do, while *Comings and Goings* does not. The basic construction block for *both* playwright and actor is the beat, those discrete units of action which make up a scene. In transformations each scene (sometimes each beat) is considered separately; there is no necessary attempt to relate one scene to the next through organic development: one scene *follows* another but does not logically grow out of it. The relationship between beats, or scenes, is para-logical or pre-logical—a relationship of free association or arbitrary cue. Thus, in *Keep Tightly Closed,* when Jaspers, Michaels, and Gregory become Custer's soldiers and an Indian Chief they are not actors playing characters who are playing other characters (as the actress playing Claire has Claire play Madame in Genet's *The Maids*), but actors playing Custer's men and the Indian directly, as if it were a separate scene entirely. The actors are cued into the soldier-Indian scene through a free association from Jaspers' suggestion of "torture" immediately before the transformation.

The three scenes are set in the matrix of the play; but the links between the scenes are not organic. One link is an association, the other a technical cue. Miss Terry is able to in-corporate transformations into the play by building into her text the same rules which govern transformations as an acting exercise. The actor's way of working and the playwright's coincide. In *Keep Tightly Closed* the characters are continu-ally being transformed into other characters, all based on the play's theme of entrapment, escape, torture, and expiation. The play develops through a set of concrete free associations. Because she worked the play out with the actors, Miss Terry had the advantage of their imaginations. In this play, as in *Viet Rock,* she maintains a real distance between herself and her creation; her "negative capability," it seems to me, is directly related to the way in which she uses her actors as part of the playwrighting process.

One can use transformations without changing the char-acters; instead, one changes the actors. This is what Miss Terry does in *Comings and Goings.* Here, between beats or in the midst of them, actors are sent in to replace other actors. Miss Terry describes the staging of the play. "A wheel was spun by a disinterested party at intervals of thirty-five to ninety seconds. A name was called out and one actor ran into the play and another actor ran out. I had originally thought the director would sit on one of the benches with the actors and send them in like a coach does at a basketball game." Thus in *Comings and Goings* the scenes may or may not develop organically. If they do not, we add to this scheme the one we saw in *Keep Tightly Closed.* As a matter of fact, *Comings and Goings* is an organic piece playing out variations on the theme of male-female love relationship. The continual changing of actors, each of whom bring their own interpretations to the part—while it is being played—means that the action will be jolted. There will be no consistent interpretation of roles. In one performance we may see dozens of ways to act the play. The action is pushed this way and that as different actors come on stage. But instead of distracting us from the action, we see its possibilities more clearly. No longer does an audience identify actor and character (such identification is impossible because the actors keep changing). Instead, most of the audience's attention is divided between the virtuosity of the group of performers (an appreciation of "pure performance") and a close scrutiny of the action which almost seems abstract when stripped of its usual actor-character identification.

Viet Rock uses both kinds of transformations. In the opening scene the actors become, in rapid sequence, a human, primordial flower, mothers and infants, army doctors and inductees, inductees and mothers. In the Senate Hearing scene actors replace other actors within the framework of a single scene. The richness of *Viet Rock* depends largely on the interweave between these two basic modes of transformation. *Viet Rock* thus develops along several lines simultaneously. If it survives the furor over the war (assuming that *we* survive), it will be because the play is a valid artwork independent of its topical references. These references are of course important—they are the concrete bricks with which Miss Terry makes her images and actions; but another set of bricks, used in the same way, would have made as attractive, if thematically different, a play. *Viet Rock* is significant first, therefore, not because it parodies and satirizes a wide range of attitudes relating to the war, but because it uses new theatrical techniques. A relatively small group of actors, trained together, assisting the playwright in every stage of the play's development, are able to portray a world of more than a hundred characters without ever seeming to "double" their roles. In fact, we lose sight of the characters as we become increasingly aware of the steady, rhythmic, and progressive flow of the action. Only a few characters stand out—the Sergeant, the Madonna, Hanoi Hannah; the rest are submerged in the experience of seeing a war scrutinized at home, in the billets, on the battlefield, off duty. This scrutiny has an extraordinary range; it is personal, domestic, political, military;

it involves the American soldiers, their families, their leaders, the North and South Vietnamese.

The theme and scope, the variety and density, of *Viet Rock* would have excited Brecht, just as Miss Terry's politics may have disappointed him. Despite the fact that those of the American Left who know *Viet Rock* have welcomed it, the play is non-political. It is a war play and as such it is an anti-war play. But it is not propagandistic or dogmatic. At two points, Miss Terry and the play's production make a political statement, both times directly to the audience. Toward the end an actress steps into the audience saying, "This war is worms. This war is worms invaded by worms. This war is eating away at the boy flesh inside my belly. This war stinks." And at the very end of the play all the actors go into the audience, confronting and touching individuals in the audience. This final gesture throws the problems of the war, its cruelty, inanity, horror, and political shortsightedness directly at the audience. But this final gesture is also elegaic and gentle, a real, physical contact between the quick and the dead, the theatre world and the worldly world. For most of the play Miss Terry represents, and disparages, *all* points of view. *Viet Rock* (like so much of Brecht) is loaded with parody and satire, echoes of popular themes and classic texts. Hollywood movies, advertising catch phrases, political speeches and attitudes, slogans of the Left, Right, and Middle, the soap opera, TV documentaries—all of these, and more, find voice and gesture in *Viet Rock*. But the play is not an exercise of sources; it has very much its own integrity.

This integrity is rooted not only in the thematic and scenic continuity and flow but also in the way Miss Terry fuses performance and text. *Viet Rock* is written, its scenes and actions are concrete, but locked into the text is the fluidity of the transformations from which the play was made. What emerges is a peculiarly powerful unit which is at once loose and tight, free and formed, massive and light. Serious scene and parody, sentimental moment and satire, brutal death and vaudeville gag are all knitted into the complex crossweave of the sudden transformations.

Miss Terry's plays—especially *Viet Rock*—justify the close cooperation between actors and playwright. Attempts in this direction—notably *Hatful of Rain*—have been disappointing before. I believe it is the addition of the transformation—a major innovation in acting and playwrighting—and Miss Terry's great skill in using transformations both as a source and product that makes this cooperative work successful now. *Viet Rock* and *Keep Tightly Closed* both have great scope and depth without claptrap. Miss Terry does not waste time relating her scenes to a realistic organic structure. She moves directly to the center of an action, and switches suddenly from action to action. She has learned how to use the accumulated imagination of the Open Theatre's actors and directors. She must still go home at night and write her scenes; but she does so in the context of the day's explorations. Her opportunities for constructive theft are multiplied. And so are the theatre's.

RICHARD SCHECHNER

New Orleans
November, 1966

VIET ROCK

∎

(*A Folk War Movie*)

PRODUCTION NOTES

∎

Viet Rock was developed in my Saturday Workshop at the Open Theatre. It grew out of improvisation, combined with the exploration of acting techniques discovered and perfected by Joseph Chaikin in his Monday Workshops.

We used material that bombarded us every day from television and newspapers. We acted out personal stories and tried to get at the roots of our drives toward anger and aggression. To deal with the bewilderment, shame, and confusion created by this war, I felt we had to explore our negative feelings, drives, and fantasies. I worked to expose these qualities, then formalized them. Also, we explored loss, grief, and regret. We tried to get at the essence of violence.

Out of the material surfacing from this work I made the play, and we began to rehearse it. Most of the staging came naturally out of the content. The director must keep in mind that the visual images here are more important than the words.

Marianne de Pury, the composer, worked with me

from the very first exercises. The music grew along with the play and is still developing.

As work progressed, we found we could get strong values by playing the scenes with an attitude of light irony. This builds a certain driving ruthlessness, which must not become heavy. If the right balance is maintained, the audience will become involved intellectually, emotionally, and kinesthetically. Audience involvement is necessary and must be there to make the play work.

Every positive and comic value in the play must be played, and then the dark values will come through with twice the impact.

I had written and designed *Viet Rock* to be played at Ellen Stewart's Café La Mama Experimental Theatre Club. This is a small, long narrow room, with low ceilings. To make maximum use of this space the audience was seated in bleacher-like formations on either side of the playing area, and some of the action takes place directly on the floor. The actors almost constantly address the audience, and this had vivid impact in such close quarters.

When we were asked to take the play to other stages and spaces like Yale, I feared the impact would be less. I was wrong. The play takes on more dimension with increase of space and audience size. The audience can't enjoy the individual actors to the same close extent, but the accumulative aspects of the play seem even more crushing on a bigger stage.

It is most necessary that the director make maximum use of his playing area and concentrate not only on the intent of the scene but the emotional content—is it being felt by the audience in how it looks to them? Lighting can be most helpful here, especially in proscenium with black curtains. It's gratifying to know that the play works no matter what the space. But one should never lose sight of the fact that it grew out of, and is, ultimately playing against world events. Some of my fellow writers berated me for not writing something more timeless. Luckily this comment did not shock me into silence.

The only scenery—two benches and four chairs. The men should be dressed in blue work clothes and boots, and the women in free-flowing dresses or skirts and tights. As many actors should be employed as the director feels confident to work with. I had from thirteen to sixteen and would have liked more.

THE SETTING:

Posted around the theatre, if the director wishes, or worked into the setting, should be the following phrases. It would be good if the audience could see them before the play begins. They should not be spotlighted or illuminated in any way. But just woven in here and there. After all, they are with us every day of this war.

Offense   Action   Yell   Freedumb   Enter
Killer Trainees   Men of Good Will   The New
Army   Viet Nam Hangs Over Your Head
The Ultimate Weapon   Victor-Charlies
Action   Freebies   Get It Over With
Bulldozer   Pow-we   Specie?   Eat   Dickhead
You Yankee?   V-C   The End Is Ongoing
Freedom   Hi Sweetheart!   Sell Out

23

Vigorous and Optimistic   Gut Hanging Out
Her Son   Racist   Your Name's on It   Flirt
with Her   Hit   Up   Out   The Up and
Down Way   Pleads   I Say Your Name Back
Play Her Game   Hawk-Dove-Owl-Worms
Our Little Yellow Brothers   Is There a
Sign?   Round Eyes   A Position in the
World   Contain   Die Away   Treesies   Win
the Balls Game   A Whole Man   Make Love
Oriental Needs Us as Enemy   Concentration
Escalation   Mouth Your Tongue   Believe
History   Deploy Tactics   Into Bed   Out
East   Pretentions   Non-White   Withdrew
Withdraw   Withdrawn   Advance   Dissent
Respectable   Hot   The Never Again Club
Playmate of the Month   Limited War   Our
Society   Your Rights   Rough Days Ahead
for Him   Alternative   Patriot   Your Turn
The Path We're On   I Have Been Wrong
Political Future   Mortal Fear   Not His Job
Half a Century Fire   His Truth Is Marching
On   Sense of Duty   Revolutionary War
War of 1812   Civil War   Indian Wars
Spanish-American War   Cave War
WWI&II&K   Love War   Stomp   Short
Order War   Words Are Actions   A Kill-In
Bombed-Out   Messages   Peace Efforts   At
Home   Wholesale Price   Index Up   A
Threat-In   Bless Your Heart   Feeding Her
People   Happening-Frustration   Hold
Debate   Length   Possible   Nastiness
Difficulty   Hawkish   Distress   Trouble

Standstill   Thrashing   Face   Belligerent
Against   Unwilling   Upset   Withdraw
Where   In the Throes   Bankrupt
Tendencies   Process   90mm Recoilless Rifle
No Time to Myself   Infant-ry   God Love Ya
One Man Cannon Balls   The Kid   Our
Commitments   Own Special Interests   Bland
Terms   Do What We Have To Do   Where
Does Your Image Hurt Now?   Practice
Dummies   The Hand of God   "Eee-ya," He
Screamed   Lost His Grip   Wanta Bite?
Peacekeeper of the World   Under Bird   No
Kidding   Put Your Lives on the Line   Hip-in
Hi Joe!   You and Yours   I Dreamed I Saw
JFK Last Night, Alive as You and Me   Never
Mind the Rain—Eat Mud   You're a Riot
Alice   I'm Too Young   What the Hell Is
That?   Prop-a-Gandhi   Reject Ancient
Quarrels   Ring Dang Doo   Accept   Honor
Zappppppppppp   Pledge   Do—For Your
Country   YER A BUNCH OF NERVOUS
NELLIES

VIET ROCK

■

(A Folk War Movie)

ACT ONE

(As audience is getting settled actors begin to appear, one by one or in pairs. They lie down on the stage. When everyone is settled there is a short silence. As lights begin to dim, song is heard on tape. It should be played once before action begins.)

MALE VOICE *(Singing The Viet Rock)*:
  Far across the Southern Sea
  Is a land where Viets rock.
  Here every morning you can see
  The Viets roll.
  When the bombs fall
  The Viets rock and rock.
  When the napalm bursts
  Then the Viets roll.
  At the sound of jets
  The Viets rock and rock.

When the tracers flash
Then the Viets roll.
Rock and roll, rock and roll,
How the sweet Viets
Love to rock and roll.
Those dear little Viets
Love our rock and roll.
Do the Viet Rock,
Watch that Viet roll.
Do the Viet Rock,
Watch that Viet roll.
That's the way the Viets rock,
All the way the Viets roll.
Rock and roll, rock and roll,
Do the Viet Rock.

(*As lights dim up, the actors are discovered lying on the floor in a circle. Their bodies, heads inward, form a giant flower or a small target. They are still; bit by bit movement can be detected. First: as if flower petals are stirred by wind or are warming toward the sun.*)

A VOICE ON TAPE (*Recites the following*): Things could be different. Nobody wins. We are teams of losers. Whatever doesn't kill you makes you stronger. Or isn't life the dream of those who are dying? It's only by virtue of our eyes that there are stars. I've been a long time a-comin' and I'll be a long time gone. Let us persevere in what we have resolved before we forget. Look out for number one. What you don't know can kill you.

(Silence. Viet Rock song is heard on tape again. Silence. From circle of bodies we hear humming or gurgling. Sound rises bit by bit, at times leaps into laughter and childlike sound of delight. The sounds should be joyous, aggressive, like those children make when playing vigorous games, but in no way should the actors try to give their impressions of sounds they think children make. This is cloying and irritating. The sound must come from their past, but the voices must come from inside and not be forced. The actors should have worked to free their imaginations before the play begins. What happens in the first ten minutes on the floor should take on the character of group free association, to represent a tribal recall of ancient scenes and events. Playtime material, especially of war games, cowboys and Indians, cops and robbers, should be allowed to come to the surface and explode into sound, sounds of weapons, horses, tanks, planes, guns, troops, orders, marching, bugles, songs, etc. The tenor of the sound should be one of joyful mastery, and imaginative striving to succeed in a frightening situation. Once the sound begins to build, the actors keep each other going: they must listen to each other. The sound should rise to climax and end in one final burst of chord sound. As the explosive sound begins to fall, they should turn on their bellies, crawl toward center, and reach out for each other. They talk to each other in

29

a bubbly way and, holding hands, slowly rise together. This makes a beautiful shape, round but changing. They keep their heads down to maintain shape. As they rise, they begin to move in a circle. The circle begins to bounce. The sound is teasing and full of fun; when they are nearly erect the circle should bounce up and down in unison. When it reaches a climax, the circle should explode, flinging the actors around the floor, laughing. They stay in place, laughing at each other.

There is an instant transformation. The male actors become new babies, and the female actors become mothers. The women find the nearest baby boy on the floor and kneel down to play with their baby. The only words they may use are "mama" and "baby." The women begin to undress the men lovingly, playing with the babies and kissing them. They continue this until all the men are stripped to their shorts. The feeling should be one of play, discovery, and contentment. As soon as he is stripped, the actor who will play the SERGEANT *in the play leaps to his feet and yells*): Ten-Hut! (*The men leap to their feet and assemble into lines for an army physical. Several women become cold, impersonal doctors and perform an examining ritual on the men. Two women sit in chairs facing the audience. As each man is okayed they look at a person in the audience and announce*): U.S. Government Inspected Male. (*The men in the line jump to two doctors. If the audience is on two sides of the action, two sets of doctors should be used. The men are commanded to jump, cough, and bend over while they receive shots. When they bend over the two doctors give them a swat. At the sound of the swat the women facing the audience make their announcement.)*

DOCTORS (*Sing*):
> Jump cough bend.

MEN (*Sing*):
> Stick him in the arm,
> Stick him in the end.   (*Repeat*)

WOMEN (*Sing*):
> U.S. Government Inspected Male!

DOCTORS (*Sing*):
> Jump cough bend.

MEN (*Sing*):
> Stick him in the arm,
> Stick him in the end.   (*Repeat*)

WOMEN (*Sing*):
> U.S. Government Inspected Male!

DOCTORS (*Sing*):
> Jump cough bend.

MEN (*Sing*):
> Stick him in the ass
> And see if he'll mend.   (*Repeat*)

31

DOCTORS (*Sing*):
> Jump cough bend.

WOMEN (*Sing*):
> U.S. Government Inspected Male!

MEN (*Sing*):
> JIGGLE HIS BALLS
> And see if he'll blend.　　　(*Repeat*)

DOCTORS (*Sing*):
> Jump cough bend.

MEN (*Sing*):
> Jump cough bend,
> Stick it in the arm
> But you'll get it in the end.　　　(*Repeat*)

WOMEN:
> U.S. Government Inspected Male!

> (*Two mothers in a coffee shop near Whitehall Street wait for their sons who are being examined for induction. They play their scene very big, very fast, seated to the side of the stage, brightly lit. A low drum beat begins.*)

MRS. SHERMAN (*Nervous and fidgety; to break her tension she tries to start a conversation*): Ah, do you have the time?

MRS. COLE (*Cold*): Yes.

MRS. SHERMAN: That's nice.

MRS. COLE: There's a clock on the wall.

MRS. SHERMAN: Oh, so there is. I didn't notice. (MRS.

COLE *shrugs and turns away.* MRS. SHERMAN'S *tension mounts.*) It's a long wait. (MRS. COLE *gives her a "what the hell do you mean?" look.* MRS. SHERMAN *nods.*) It's such a long wait in a short time like this. (MRS. COLE *turns away.*) I can't stand to think of him in there with all the rest of them, being treated like a peace of meat. (MRS. COLE *turns more severely away.*) How old is your boy?

MRS. COLE: I beg your pardon?

MRS. SHERMAN: Your son?

MRS. COLE: What?

MRS. SHERMAN: I, oh, excuse me, I thought you were waiting for your son like I am.

MRS. COLE: I'm drinking coffee.

MRS. SHERMAN: I'm sorry, but I'm nervous. Aren't you nervous?

MRS. COLE: Why should I be nervous?

MRS. SHERMAN: Well, if your boy was being examined by the army this very minute, wouldn't you be nervous?

MRS. COLE: He is.

MRS. SHERMAN: But you said you were only drinking coffee.

MRS. COLE: I am. (MRS. SHERMAN *gives her a bewildered look.*) They won't take him.

Mrs. Sherman: Something wrong with him?

Mrs. Cole: There's nothing wrong with him. He's perfect.

Mrs. Sherman: Oh yeah?

Mrs. Cole (*Looking at watch*): He should be here any minute. It won't take them long to make up their minds.

Mrs. Sherman: You got pull, eh?

Mrs. Cole: They wouldn't take my Laird. He'd be terrible in a jungle.

Mrs. Sherman: I know they'll take Ralphie. I just know it. He's built fifty forts on our fire escape. He knows everything about building forts.

Mrs. Cole: That'll come in handy.

Mrs. Sherman: He'll be protecting the freedom of your son.

Mrs. Cole: Some have to go.

Mrs. Sherman: He'll be fighting for your little boy.

Mrs. Cole: I can't help that. God didn't designate my Laird to be a fighter.

Mrs. Sherman: You do it for him, eh?

Mrs. Cole: The strong have to protect the weak.

Mrs. Sherman: It isn't fair. My Ralphie's A-1, er 1-A. He was such a little baby. You wouldn't believe. He only weighed four pounds and two ounces when he was born. Such an easy birth. It was my husband gave all the trouble. We had to run to the hospital. The car wouldn't start. Ralphie was born in the emergency receiving room. He wouldn't wait. (MRS. COLE *looks up to see her son coming toward her. While this happens the other men continue dressing at one side of the stage.*)

LAIRD: Hi hi hi, M-M-M-M-Mom.

MRS. COLE: Laird. What the hell are you wearing?

LAIRD: I'm I'm I'm I'm . . .

MRS. COLE: No.

LAIRD: Yes.

MRS. COLE: They wouldn't.

LAIRD (*Smiling*): M-M-M-M-M-M-Mom, I made it.

MRS. COLE: But how could they?

LAIRD: They like me, M-M-M-M-M-Mom, I'mmmm All Am-Am-Am-American.
(MRS. SHERMAN *sees* RALPHIE *come toward her.*)

RALPHIE: Hi, Mom.

MRS. COLE (*Hugging* LAIRD *and crying*): Oh, Baby . . .

MRS. SHERMAN: Ralphie! (*She pulls him to her.*) Tell me?

RALPHIE: It's O.K., Mom. Mom, there was this guy in there he was so . . . Oh . . . (*Seeing* LAIRD *in his mother's arms*) There he is! They're getting desperate, Mom . . . but . . .

MRS. SHERMAN: Something's wrong. Tell me. Ralphie, I can feel it. . . .

RALPHIE (*Kisses her on the cheek*): I'm going to be all right. I just have to go to the hospital a couple days.

MRS. SHERMAN: Oh Ralphie, you have blood in your urine! You have blood in your urine!

RALPHIE: I'm in the army. It's O.K. I'll just have to go to the hospital a couple of days.

MRS. SHERMAN (*Hugging and kissing* RALPHIE): You get rid of that blood. (*Sings*):

Now that you are up so tall
I have to share you with the world,
But I can't be nice all the time,
I get mad and up comes my gall.

Goodbye, my good boy,
Goodbye, my good boy.
Go quick,
Mother promised not to cry.

But if you have to go
I got to give you strength.
I won't chicken out
And I won't shrink.

But I don't like it,
Why can't I fight it?

Goodbye, my good boy,
Goodbye, my dear,
Goodbye, my good boy,
Mother holds you here.

I lost too many already
And now it comes again.
But I don't like it,
Why can't I fight it?

The wars have melted into one,
A war was on when I was born.
Will this be on when I am done?
That kind of triple feature, please God save
    me from.

Goodbye, my good boy,
Goodbye, my love,
Goodbye, my good boy, I wish you weren't
    old enough.

RALPHIE: Goodbye, Mom. (RALPHIE *then kisses* MRS.
COLE *goodbye. All the other male actors line
up to kiss* MRS. SHERMAN *goodbye. They each
make a different character adjustment to her.
Then they all kiss* MRS. COLE *goodbye. They
kiss all the females goodbye. The women doctors have now turned into mothers or sweethearts and sit on benches. While this action
takes place one woman sings to the audience
while sitting on a chair. As the song ends the*
SERGEANT *yells.*)

SERGEANT: Fall in. Ten-hut! (*The men get into an awkward line. The* SERGEANT *snaps them up. The following should be an accelerated drill course.*) I hate recruits! Now listen, you mens, and listen good. The army is going to train you mens to become ultimate weapons. Is that clear? (*The men nod.*) Is that *clear?* (*They nod again. This makes the* SERGEANT *very angry.*) Answer me like you got a pair!

GI's (*Scream*): Yes, Sergeant! (SERGEANT *is satisfied.*)

SERGEANT (*Continuing his drill course*): Left face. Right face. About face. Right face! (*The men make mistakes and the* SERGEANT *corrects them with tense enjoyment.*) Left face, right face. About face. Right face. About face. (*One of the men does not please him. He calls him out of line.*) You, Allen, get out here. The rest of you men watch. (*The men rush to watch. The* SERGEANT *is angry.*) Fall in! In place—watch! Don't move! Don't move, girls. Allen. In place march! (*He marches in stylized fashion. The* SERGEANT *is almost nose to nose with him.*) Allen, in place double time. (*He marches faster and faster.*) Company halt, one two. (*The soldier makes one more foot fall than he should and the* SERGEANT *glares him back to his place.*) Fall in. In place march. Left face, in place march. About face. Right face. (*He gets them back facing him.*) All right, girlies, you're in the army now. Sound off!

GI's: One two.

SERGEANT: Sound off!

GI's: Three, four.

SERGEANT: Cadence count.

GI's: One two three four, one-two, three-four!

SERGEANT: O.K. Girlies, forward march! (*They march around the stage as he eyes them carefully.*) Company halt! Very good, girlies. One day you'll become ladies. Ten-hut. O.K., girlies, we're going to do some push-ups. At ease. Fall into place. (*The men fall down in push-up positions.*) One. Two. Three. Four. Five.

(SERGEANT *fades back to watch their form. During the push-up formation, the man speaking the line is up, and the others are flat against the floor. They should go up and down when their line comes up.*)

GI ONE: You know that all young men have to face a time in life when they have to make their own decisions. When they have to put Momma's voice aside and when they have to face up.

GI TWO: Well, that time came to me, that time that all young men must face up to.

GI THREE: This is the time that I call the breaking point.

GI FOUR: This is the time when the young man puts away childish things, like childhood and Mom-

39

ma's voice so that he can step out into the world a man.

GI FIVE: I chose to make my own foot felt by walking through the door of the induction center.

GI SIX: That's what I call marking my breaking point.

GI SEVEN: I didn't have to get anybody's O.K., no names signed beside my one.

GI EIGHT: It was my thing to do.

GI ONE: So I put my foot down on the threshold to manhood and put away my childhood.

GI TWO: And now as I go through life, I . . .

(*All men are up in top of push-up position for this speech.*)

ALL GI'S:

. . . Pray to my sergeant that I may be a man to man.

I pray to my sergeant that I may be a man to sergeant.

I pray to my sergeant that I may be a man to country.

I pray to my sergeant that I may be a man to Mother.

I pray to my sergeant that I may be a man to Dog.

I pray to my sergeant that I may be a man to God.

SERGEANT: All right, girls. Ten-hut! (*He sings to them*):

(*WAR AU GO GO*)

Come my ladies, take your rifles
Here my bunnies are grenadies,
Stand to battle,
Little pussies.
War au go go
Is our game.

That's my sweethearts, War au go go,
Get your back up,
War au go go,
War au go go
Is our game.

Come, my girlies,
Suck in your tummies
To win your stripies,
Act like ladies,
Because it's war au go go
For my girlies.
War au go go
For my babes.
War au go go, War au go go,
War au go go
Is our game.

Grip your rifles, little bunnies,
Throw grenadies, little ladies.
Run to battle,
Little pussies.
War au go go
Is our game.

> War au go go, little honeys,
> War au go go,
> Smarten up, you dames!
> War au go go,
> War au go go,
> War au go go,
> Is our game.
>
> War au go go!

> (*Everyone comes in on "War au go go's."*)

SERGEANT: All right, ladies. Fall in! Ten-hut! (*He sings*):

> You're in the army now,
> You're not atop a cow . . .

GI's AND WOMEN (*Sitting on benches*):

> You'll never get rich,
> You son-of-a-bitch,
> You're in the shit-house now!

SERGEANT: Sound off!

GI's: One two.

SERGEANT: Sound off.

GI's: Three four.

SERGEANT: Cadence count.

GI's: One two three four, one-two, three-four!

> (*The* SERGEANT *inspects them and might slap or snap at one whose button is wrong, etc.*)

Ten-hut! Forward march! (*They march across the stage, filling it. They reach the other side.*)

SERGEANT (*Yells*): Halt. Left Face. (*As they do, all the female actors with arms linked rush on and fall down in a kneeling position ranged across center stage.*) About face, forward march. (*As the men make an about-face and march forward, they stumble over the women. Muffled sounds of* "Broads! Hey, Sarge, look at these lovelies," *etc.*)

GI ONE: Hi, darlin! (*He grabs a girl.*) You come to see me off? (*He stoops to kiss her.*)

SERGEANT (*Pulling him off by seat of his pants and throwing him back into the line*): That's a protester, you dogbody, you piss-headed lassie!

GI ONE: She ain't mine? Sergeant!

SERGEANT (*Slapping him*): Straighten up and shut up, girlie!

HEAD PROTESTER (*At end of line, she lifts her head and calls out to the* SERGEANT): Sir, I hereby inform you that you are hereby under citizen's arrest by a citizen of these United States. You are charged, sir, with genocide, criminal conspiracy, and carrying on a full-scale war under the guise of an "expeditionary force."

SERGEANT: Take that pink mitt off this Government property.

PROTESTER: If you will come quietly, sir, I can guarantee

you the same fair trial that was conducted in Nuremberg and Israel.

SERGEANT: You are bruising $250,000 worth of Government training and experience. I suggest you lie down there with your friends where we can crush you all at once.

PROTESTER: "Let you hear me gentle cousin, Westmoreland." Listen, Dog Tag number 1077866, I have arrested you in the name of morality, Christianity, and sanity!

(SERGEANT *looks at protesters and starts laughing. He goes down his line of men and digs each one in ribs till each man laughs at women during their chanting.*)

HEAD PROTESTER: Citizen's arrest . . . !

ALL PROTESTERS: Stop the war in Vietnam. Make love, not war. BRING OUR BOYS HOME. Stop the war in Vietnam. Make love, not war. Bring our boys home. Stop the war in Vietnam. Make love, not war. Bring our boys home. . . .

SERGEANT (*Shouting at protesters*): You aren't worth me stomping my boot on. The army is the instrument of the will of the people. That's "consensus" to you, mushheads. Go back to U. S. History 101. Have you forgotten the Indian Wars already? What country are you really from?

(*While the* SERGEANT *has been saying the above speech, three of the women protesters have left the line of women and have taken up a position elsewhere on stage. During the following they mime pouring gasoline on themselves and light a real wooden match.*)

PROTESTERS (*Kneeling with arms linked, they face the soldiers*): We ask you to stop this merciless war.

GI's (*Shouting as if answering a superior officer*): We didn't start it!

PROTESTERS: Innocent people on all sides are being maimed and murdered.

GI's (*Shouting*): Sorry about that!

PROTESTERS: Homes are destroyed and people uprooted.

GI's: Downright sorry about that!

PROTESTERS: Join us and stay home.

GI's: We'd like to stay home, but we must serve.

PROTESTERS: Innocent people are being burned.

GI's: Gee, we really are sorry about that!

PROTESTERS: Is that your final answer?

GI's: We have a job to do. There can be no questions.

(*The three women strike the wooden matches, whip the lighted matches up and down. The matches go out, and the women are burned. They fall to the floor, jerking and moaning, in final stages of death. The* GI's *stand stiffly at attention. The* SERGEANT *is furious.*)

45

SERGEANT (*To men*): What you standing with yer faces hanging out, ladies? Police the area! On the double! (*Men brutally drag all the women to the benches and throw them down. Women quietly take sitting position on benches while the men start to grind the ashes from the bodies of the three into the ground the way they'd try to get rid of cigarette ashes inadvertently dropped on their mothers' rugs.*) Fall in! Ten-hut! (*GI's form up into the ultra-erect straight line. At the* SERGEANT'S *nod, one by one they jump out of line and address the audience.*)

GI ONE: What a pity it is that we have what you can apply to some guys the implication "draft dodger." (*He jumps back to place.*)

GI TWO (*Jumping out*): Some of these dodgers even burn their bodies and cards of the draft.

GI THREE: I believe some of these activities are called "protest moves."

GI FOUR: Now I ask you, how could our forefathers who bled all over this ground that I'm standing on here, how could they not roll around in the hallowed ground of their graves?

GI FIVE: I ask you?

GI SIX: These here are immature actions of these so-called American youth.

GI SEVEN: If our forefathers heard about this, they'd grab up their rusty muskets and rise up from their graves and shoot down the whole bunch of these here so-called American youths who are protesting our so-called Vietnam war.

GI EIGHT: These aren't so-called youths.

GI ONE: These are sneaking subversive commies, that's what they are.

GI FOUR: I suggest to these so-called guys they should take some time off from their burning and do a little deep study of this here problem like I've paid attention to it.

GI TWO: If they won't I suggest we put 'em on a fast boat to Commie China.

GI THREE: I'll pay half the fare myself.

GI FIVE: Just because you don't . . .

GI SIX: . . . Agree with your country . . .

GI SEVEN: . . . Doesn't mean you shouldn't . . .

GI EIGHT: . . . Do what they tell you to.

ALL (*Jumping out*): And that's all I have to say to these so-called youths.

SERGEANT (*He turns to address the audience*): These punks, these commies, these bleeding hearts. They're so dumb, they're tools of the pinko-reds. These guys who claim to be pacifists—these—they are consumed by war. Do you see them fighting against cancer? No, they're consumed with making exhibits of themselves. Do you see them throwing their bodies down in

47

front of the Detroit assembly lines? That's where some bellyaching is needed. I'd help them protest the frigging motorcars. Ain't a one of them that's not more deadly every day actually than the myth of the BOMB. More bastards bleed their guts out and grind their bones on the cement of our highways than ever lose a piece of snot in Vietnam. These punks is consumed with war. They are against war. Methinks they protest too much. They're scared if they had a legal gun in their hands they'd blow off every head in sight. Maybe their own. They're a bunch of potential suicides and they work it off by protesting us, and making out they're smarter than us, and more humanitarian and such. Let me ask you where we'd all be if we hadn't fought in World War I, World War II, and Korea? Dead in our beds. That's where. You punks wouldn't even a been a gleam in yer old man's eye, 'cause yer old man woulda been dead before he could get it up. They should get out and fight and get it out of their guts. Since when is it not honorable to die for your country? Spill your blood, boobies. That's the highest form of love. Give your blood for others. These guys is afraid to look at war. You have to fight now to prevent the big one. These crybabies who're 'fraid of the bomb are asking for it. Thank God there's some men left in America. These bleeding hearts are afraid to look at death. Death ain't so bad. It's very, very peaceful. I mean real death, with real guts strewn about the ground. Real ashes of real houses burned to the dirt. Real skulls buried in the dirt with just the few teeth left to grin up at the sun. Baby bodies dotting the dirt like bean sprouts in chow mein. I ain't afraid to look. Slant-eyed mommas crying over the limp remains of black-haired sons. I seen it all. I seen it all. Let the crybabies stay home and hide in their moms' closets and wipe themselves with apple pie. No wars on foreign soils to quiver their weak little crotches. I don't want any one of them what's so tied up in a death struggle with his own dad that he can't go out and be a man and defend his home. I wouldn't want him in my platoon. Yes, boys. War is hell. And you have to be a hell of a man, with a hell of a lot of blood to spill for the hell of a lot of love you have for your hell of a country! Get aboard now and know that the U.S.A. is behind you all the way. Ten thousand miles right here behind you. We'll show your dead brothers in arms that they did not have died in vain. God love ya, and go get that guy, before he gets you first. For God. For country. For the land of the brave and the home of the free. Fall in! (*The men fall into single file led by the* SER-GEANT *and march in place as the female actors come on stage in concentrated force with rising sounds to form an airplane. The men march down and around the airplane, then halt.*) All right, ladies, prepare to go abroad. Next stop,

Vietnam! (*The* SERGEANT *supervises the men boarding the plane. The men enter, stand in middle of plane, attach their parachute cords, and face each other in two rows. The sound of the plane changes to one of take-off, the plane then levels off. The sound changes from that of an engine to one of spirits, high, but sweet. The plane arrives in Asia. The female actors melt away but stay concentrated. The men are left in a cluster on stage.*) All right, ladies, bail out! (*The men bail out one at a time. Some have to be pushed by the* SERGEANT. *They yell, then count as they jump.*)

GI's: 1001, 1002, 1003, 1004, 1005, 1006.

(*The chutes open, and they enjoy floating to earth. If the men move their feet very little, but feel the pull of gravity in their hips and thighs and steer the chutes with their arms, the effect can be quite touching.*)

SERGEANT (*Bails out and shouts*): Satchmo! Satchmo! Satchmo!

(*The GI's say their lines to the audience as they float down to earth.*)

GI ONE: I didn't prepare myself.

GI TWO: The clouds look like whipped potatoes.

GI THREE: That sergeant is as helpful as a bag full of holes.

GI FOUR: When I get home, I'm gonna make people stop and think.

GI FIVE: There, I'm getting my own individual style.

GI SIX: I wish Tuesday Weld could see me now.

GI SEVEN: When I catch her, I'm gonna kiss the daylights out of her.

GI EIGHT: This gives me tingles in my tummy.

GI ONE: I'd like to tell you that having been raised in a small and sheltered town, this is like going from one world into another.

GI TWO: Will I pass the test of life?

GI THREE: I can't wait to get there and make a killing in the black market.

GI FOUR: I'm making a career in the army because I just can't wait until the next day arrives so that I can see what interesting things are going to happen to me next.

GI FIVE: I joined the service to get some time to think.

GI SIX: Gee, it's a nice day. . . .

GI SEVEN: John Wayne has faith in me.

GI EIGHT: Whores don't kiss.

GI ONE: I'm the greatest!

> (*The plane has overshot the Vietnam border and deposited our boys in Shangri-la. The*

SERGEANT *had landed beyond them. One of
the actors quickly buries his chute, then climbs
a bench to represent a mountain ridge, and
assumes the carriage of the high* LAMA. *The
other* GI's *pull down their chutes, quickly bury
them, and when they see the high* LAMA *approach, they crouch with their guns drawn.*)

LAMA (*Bowing*): Kama Sutra, Kemo Sabe! Siddartha
has crossed the Rhine. Kissed the women and
drinked the wine. The deep blue sea washes
you and me. What is salt without stew? And
the sound of one hand stealing is the shot heard
around the world. While sojourning in our
hidden paradise—enjoy, enjoy! Drink from
our springs of happiness. Wash your GI socks
in our fountain of foolishness. Become as
little children and the Rat Race wrinkles will
fade from your tongue. (*He bows and our
boys bow back. Gong.*) You have arrived at
the Holy Hiding Place of all our sons. (*He
bows and our boys bow back. Gong.*) Allah
has provided Buddha for all you sweet little
white Jesuses. Feel free to rest in the arms of
our mother bodies and trace your names on
the breasts of time. Welcome to Shangri-la!
(*The gong sounds. He bows to them and our
boys bow back. He goes back across the bench
and sits. As the last gong sounds the women
enter as Shangri-la maidens. They sing in a
high, sweet falsetto. The* "yea yea" *lines they
take to the audience.*)

WOMEN:

>Welcome to Shangri-la.
>Yea yea, welcome to Shangri-la yea yea (*to audience*).
>Give us your Yankee Hand,
>Jump into Love's quicksand,
>Welcome to Shangri-la.
>Yea yea (*to audience*).

>Here you will drink of love,
>Here you'll be raped by doves,
>Welcome to Shangri-la.
>Oh yea yea, welcome to Shangri-la (*to audience*).
>Shangri—Shangri—Yeah!

>(*They begin a slow-motion orgy with our boys.*)

SERGEANT (*Can be heard in the distance calling*): Alice Company? Alice Company? Alice Company? (*He spots the orgy.*) Aha! Aha! Aha! Aha! Aha! All right, you Little Bo Peeps! Ten-hut! Ten-hut! Ten-hut! I'll have you shot for AWOL. Let go a' the tits of human kindness and fall in! We got a job to do for our folks back home. Come on, you girls you, rise up. We have to get the freedom ringing. We can just make the jungle by the time the snow melts. Goddammit, you dogbodies! Pull up your pants and let's mush! Er, marsh. Forward. Mush.

GI ONE: Sir, just five more minutes!

SERGEANT: Ten-hut! (*The frightened platoon jumps to its feet. They straighten their clothes. The maidens follow, clinging to them. The maidens get in line behind the men.*) Fall in! Ten-hut! Let's go, on the double. We have a job to do and we're not even at the right address yet.

(*They start to march. The women learn the step quickly and all march in single file around the stage. As they march they burst into a marching song*):

To the jungle march
Through the jungle gore,
To the jungle march
Through the jungle roar.

We're off to fight for Vietnam,
We will display our might.
We're off to win for Vietnam,
We're fighting for what's right.

To bring the girls of Vietnam
To be free as we.
To make the boys of Vietnam
As free as the U.S.A.

To the jungle march
Through the jungle gore,
To the jungle march
Through the jungle roar.

(*A wild frug can be interspersed with the march. Or the march turns into a brief, high-*

spirited polka. Or the frug can be combined and choreographed and the ensemble can end in a lunatic war machine by the final stanza. They yell and step and kick. The dance ends. There is an immediate transformation and each person takes on the character he is to be first in the next scene. They crowd around one actor who seems to be preventing them from entering a room. They burst through, settle down, and we are in a Senate Investigating Committee room. The actors should take turns being senators and witnesses; the transformations should be abrupt and total. When the actor finishes with one character he becomes another, or just an actor. When not senators or witnesses they are the audience to the proceedings and take their places on benches to the side of the stage. They react in character to what transpires. There are reporters, photographers, etc. Everything must be pantomimed throughout the play.)

SENATOR ONE *(Begins quickly)*: I will make my opening remarks as brief as possible. The situation is grave, the perils immense. We hope with the aid of the Almighty to find a just, equitable, and profitable solution. May I call the first witness?

WITNESS ONE
(Is in place facing the SENATORS. *He has brought a chair from the sidelines to the center of the stage.)*

SENATOR TWO (*To Witness*): Good morning, sir.

WITNESS ONE: Good morning, sir . . . er, sirs.

SENATOR ONE: Do be seated, sir.

WITNESS ONE: Thank you, sir . . . er, sirs. I am sitting.

SENATOR TWO: Sir, let me tell the people of America that we're very pleased to have a man of your caliber and illustrious career come forward to express his view on our position in . . . er . . . in . . . er (SENATOR ONE *whispers to him*) . . . Vietnam . . .

WITNESS ONE: I see it as my duty, sir.

SENATOR ONE: Are you ready to express your views, sir?

WITNESS ONE: Yes, sir . . . er, sirs. . . . With all due respect to our Administration to whose commander and chief I am most loyal to, but sirs, it is time, I believe, that we stop pussy-footing around and won that war. From my vast experience in invading both islands and mainlands, with both foot soldiers and advanced weaponry, I say we have to lay our cards on the line and do the job. I say, get the atomic bulldozer operational. Get it off the drawing board and out bulling down that jungle. The native population should be moved temporarily to some valley in eastern California, and then get the hell the atomic bulldozer in there and push the jungle into the sea. That way there won't be any cover for the enemy to hide out in, we mop up, blacktop the cleared land—and then shazam!—we have a hell of a parking lot for jet bombers for when the next domino threatens to fall.

SENATOR ONE: Well thought out.

WITNESS ONE: Someone had to do it, sir.

SENATOR TWO: Next witness.

SENATOR ONE: You did it, sir.

WITNESS ONE: Thank you, sir.

SENATOR TWO: Next witness.

> WITNESS TWO (*grand old American Woman Statesman, starts to make her way to the witness chair. The* SENATORS *rush to help her settle herself, then they resume their seats. She looks around and smiles and tries to wave. Looks back at* SENATORS, *forgets what she's there for.*)

SENATOR TWO: An unexpected pleasure. How grand to see you again.

> (WITNESS TWO *nods and smiles.*)

SENATOR ONE: Madam, the United States, as you know, is in a sort of a pickle. And we would relish your views on our position in Vietnam.

WITNESS TWO: People—of—America! (*Applause from spectators*) When—Mr. Thant—and—I—last —spoke—we were still saying—that—it— should be entrusted—to—the U.N. How else can World—Law—take hold—to—People of

America? I—implore you—to—support—the United Nations of the World. . . . (*Applause. The two men who have been* SENATORS *rush to the witness, pick her up, and carry her to her seat. As this happens two new* SENATORS *take the chairs.*)

SENATOR ONE: Thank you, thank you, thank you. That was most . . . Next witness!

WITNESS THREE (*A prize fighter takes the stand*): The greatest. That's me. Yeah, yeah, oh yeah. The greatest and the prettiest and the sweetest that you'll ever see. Yeah, yeah, oh yeah. Oh yeah.

SENATOR TWO: What is your position on our position in Vietnam?

WITNESS THREE: To a neutral corner you should retire, before all our pretty boys and cute tiny friends all expire.

SENATOR ONE: Will the witness please be clearer?

WITNESS THREE: My good name I will lend, your ear for to bend. Two thousand X is my name. Turn it around and it's still the same. Oh yeah. Yeah, yeah. Oh yeah.

SENATOR TWO (*To* SENATOR ONE): A perfect specimen.

WITNESS THREE: Yeah, yeah, oh yeah. I'm the prettiest. I'm the greatest, and I ratest with the girls. And to stay this way, I want to say; we got no quarrel with the northern race. And that's the place where I stand. And I'm grand. And

I'm grand, man. Yeah, yeah, oh yeah. I am grand, man. Strike up the band.

SENATOR TWO: Next witness.

SENATOR ONE: We're grateful for your presence here today, sir. As a highly placed and trusted high-ranking high Government official and a high-ranking source of high information, state the latest official views, please.

WITNESS FOUR: Fellow officials . . . honored Senators . . . ladies and gentlemen of the press . . . my American fellows and gals, I want to tell you that this Administration to which I am a party to indulges in nothing but realism. I want to go on to say that realism does not rule out the hope that hope could come in the not too distant future. . . . With calculated fluctuations, however . . .

SENATOR TWO: Sir, would you care to elaborate on However?

WITNESS FOUR: Why, Senator, I'd be glad to. If the ignorant and sensational press would just stop overreacting, we could get a job of hope really done around this globe. But no! Every tiny mistake, a few teensy bundles of bombs dropped in the wrong place, and the ignorant and sensational press just has to blow every-thing up. Blow it up. Blow it up. Blow it up. Bleep it. Blop. Bleep, gleep, blow. Sleep, sleep, sleep. Forgive me, but I haven't had any sleep in eighteen months. Blow it up. Blup. Blup.

(*He falls into arms of usher who takes him to bench.*)

WITNESS FIVE (*A very neat and efficient man rushes to the stand*): Senators, sirs, may I explain what my colleague meant . . .

SENATORS: We hope so.

WITNESS FIVE (*He speaks quite rapidly like a mechanical man*): I want to assure *you*, sirs, and interested observers around the galaxy that we've begun to turn the tide. The moon is with us, we're not quite over the hump, but don't swallow the first deliberate propaganda line you see, but as free men learn to assess words. Words don't mean what they say. Actually the north is tactically defeated, but we haven't begun to see the end of this thing. Some of my colleagues are encouraged, some see a war of attrition, some are optimistic. And I'd like to say that for myself, I'm cautiously optimistic in my transistors and capacitors, but on certain days my entire circuit is in deep despair. There is a question that I'd like to put to you, sirs?

SENATORS: Why, thank you, sir. It's an honor.

WITNESS FIVE: Sirs: who is man?

SENATORS: Next witness!

WITNESS SIX (*Rushes to take her place—a volatile, upset, intense woman*): I won't stop. I won't shut up. I will not keep quiet.

SENATOR TWO: Who's this?

SENATOR ONE: Not on the schedule.

WITNESS SIX: You must negotiate with all parties. Haven't you learned the lesson of assasination?

SENATORS: Assasination?

WITNESS SIX: *You* had my husband and brother-in-law killed and *they* had your President assasinated. In some circles that is called an eye for an eye, in others tit for tat.

SENATORS: This woman is in contempt. Arrest her!

WITNESS SIX: Hanoi is a beautiful city. I was born there. I want my children to see the streets where I walked as a girl. No one is safe! No one is safe.

(*She rushes to a bench and seems to stab everyone sitting there. They slump over. She becomes only an actor again and takes her place on opposite bench. A moment of chaos.*)

SENATOR TWO: Arrest. Order? Order? Order!

SENATOR ONE: Next witness.

(WITNESS SEVEN, *a curly-headed writer, slumps to the chair and sits on the back of it.*)

SENATOR TWO: It is indeed an honor to have a writer of your intense commitment take time off from his typewriter to give his views.

SENATOR ONE: What do you think we should do about the war in Vietnam?

61

WITNESS SEVEN: Nothing.

SENATOR TWO: Nothing?

WITNESS SEVEN: Nothing. The war will die of cancer. You'll die of cancer. Everyone will die of cancer. Me, I think too much. I'll die of cerebral hemorrhage.

SENATOR ONE: Nevertheless, as a leading writer of our country we'd be happy to hear if you possibly have a possible solution.

WITNESS SEVEN: The war ain't there, it's here. It's right here now, here and now. Mark those words carefully. I said mark them. That's all there is. That's what's happening, baby! It's here and now, here and now. You and me. Between you and me and me and me and you and you and you and you and me and you and you and me. That's all that's happening, baby. Wise up before it's already happened to you. Check it out, baby, before they up-chuck you —into oblivion, baby. The war ain't there, it's right here, here and now in this obscene, cancerous glare of the TV lights and tranquilized television dinners. Television, the tremendous masterbator of the masses. Vomit up the lard, you asses, before the future of our sperm is burned in Asiatic light. All you studs got to stop smearing napalm on the genitals of the weak. We got the fever. We don't got prosperity, we got the fever. Purge the bestial disease of the computer madness wiggled into

your shit by the bitch Goddess—burn out the
blood of the malignant cells and cleanse your
ego before it's too late. The horror from the
sewer of our disease is rising up to choke your
throat and all our images are manipulated
from birth to death by cynics. Yeah boys, get
out there and bomb the bomb before you die
of cancer or you'll eat the fire next time!
Madness leaped up! Madness leaped up and
stomped on our hearts. Into oblivion baby. (*He
is dragged to a bench by two ushers.*)

SENATOR ONE: Next witness!

(WITNESS EIGHT *is an Indian who does a
controlled but violent dance to the witness
chair, chanting a Peyote Song.*)

SENATOR TWO: I beg your pardon?

WITNESS EIGHT (*After pause*): Song of my people.

SENATOR TWO: Can you give the nation, your nation's
view of the situation in Vietnam?

WITNESS EIGHT (*After a long pause, a shadow of a
smile. He gathers himself up and, shaking
from within, fires at them*): This is the end
of the line for you—and all you white men.
The red man and the yellow man and the black
man are banding together. We will run you off
the scorched face of this earth. We will run you
into the sea. We will fly you into the air. Your
turn to sing now, white man. (*He starts for
his place on the bench slowly, looking at the*

63

SENATORS, *with each phrase.*) Goodbye, white man. White man! White man!

(WITNESS NINE, *several Vietnamese women, crying softly, go to kneel before the* SENATORS. *They plead and cry. Their hands flutter in bewilderment.*)

SENATOR TWO: What have we here, Senator?

SENATOR ONE: They're Vietnamese. Thought it only democratic we ask the opinion of the common people over there.

SENATOR TWO: Good man, Senator, good man.

(WITNESSES' *crying mounts. The* SENATORS *try to pacify them.*)

SENATOR ONE: Hush now.

SENATORS (*Uncomfortably*): It won't have been in vain. We promise you . . .

SENATOR ONE: Your men have not died in vain.

SENATOR TWO: Wait'll you see the swell schools and the great highways and turnpikes we're going to build in your jungle.

SENATOR ONE: It won't be a jungle any more.

SENATOR TWO: Why, why you know what we'll do to make it up to you? We'll turn the whole damn Mekong Delta into another TVA!

SENATOR ONE: What do you think about that? (*They cry louder. The* SENATOR *rises and gestures.*)

Er, Usher! Usher, will you please escort these ladies to the powder room. I think they want to freshen up. (*The* WITNESSES *rise and quietly resume their seats. A beautiful woman,* WITNESS TEN *has taken her place in the witness chair. She arranges herself and maintains a radiant pose. The* SENATORS *rise in an attitude of prayer. Those on the benches kneel in place. Some sing, and others chant. The* SENATORS *move to the seated woman, genuflect, and place some small coins in her open palm. They genuflect again and back toward their chairs.*) Madonna, words cannot express the pleasure we feel in your presence.

SENATOR TWO: Madonna, what is your position on Vietnam?

(*The* MADONNA *carefully and slowly strikes and holds another pose. The actress playing this role should study famous paintings and sculptures of the Madonna and Child. She should choose four that suit her and that are clear to the audience. The* SENATORS *ask her three more times to state her position on Vietnam.*)

SENATOR ONE (*Chanting*): Holy Mother, we thank you for your views.

(*The* MADONNA, *gracefully and maintaining a pose, exits to her place on the bench, but it would be nice if she flew straight up and out of sight.*)

SENATOR TWO: Next witness!

WITNESS ELEVEN (*A serene-faced, beautiful man approaches. He makes a sign and steps over the chair and continues to benches on other side of stage and makes a sign of blessing*): Bless you. Bless you. Bless you.

SENATOR TWO: What is your statement, sir?

WITNESS ELEVEN: Love, brother.

SENATOR ONE (*Who should be a woman by now*): Love?

WITNESS ELEVEN: Love, sister.

SENATOR ONE: Did you say Love?

WITNESS ELEVEN: Love, daughter . . .

SENATOR ONE: Love . . .?

WITNESS ELEVEN: Love . . . Mother . . .

SENATOR ONE (*Approaches the witness with a hypnotized smile*): Love?

WITNESS ELEVEN: Love.

SENATOR ONE (*Gently touching the heart of the* WITNESS): Yeah, Love.

WITNESS ELEVEN: If you do not love—father and I will walk away. You're on your own. Love. Love or perish. (*He leaves and walks upstage where he stands with his back to the audience. Other people in the room begin to kiss, shake hands, sit with their arms around each other. Every-*

one becomes engaged in overt loving. One
couple sends love out to the audience.)

SENATOR ONE (*In a daze, walks back to her chair*):
Love. (*She kisses* SENATOR TWO.)

WITNESS TWELVE (*A vigorous contemporary patriot*
jumps up and runs to the witness chair):
What is this soft-headed, lily-livered kind of
thinking? Is this for patriots? Love can't stop
criminals or tyrants. Love is no good without
a body to express it. Get out there and defend
the right to happiness of our brothers. (*He*
leaps up on the chair.) We went across the
Atlantic to fight for freedom. Are you frightened to cross the Pacific? (*Crowd reacts,* "No,
No!") The world has shrunk to the size of a
pea. We are our brother's keeper. The flag
of the United States of America shall shelter
all who wish our aid. Hold your tongue. Stiffen
your spine. There is still something worth
fighting and worth dying for. The same thing
our fathers and grandfathers fought and died
for at Valley Forge, Gettysburg, the Alamo,
Anzio, Guadalcanal, Iwo Jima, Okinawa, Pork
Chop Hill. (*The crowd is all around his chair*
now.) Freedom. Let freedom ring! Kill for
freedom! (*The crowd repeats. He starts to*
sing "America the Beautiful.")

(*Everyone sings with genuine patriotic fervor.*
They hoist him on their shoulders. They march
all over the committee room. They march

67

*straight toward the audience, stop short, do
an about-face. Salute, hold hands on hearts,
etc. For one full chorus, then march out on
the second one. They should sing with all the
genuine love and gusto they can muster. Big,
big, big.)*

ACT TWO

*(Open with the stage filled by all the actors;
it should have the feeling of irregular squares.
Some face audience. Some face stage left,
others stage right. Some face up-stage. They
sing "America" exuberantly as before, but no
sound comes out. [If a proscenium stage is
used, begin a Rockette chorus line and kick
all the way to stage front.] Every two lines they
do an exact about-face so that they are facing
opposite direction from opening of act. When
they reach the chorus, they march to the formation for the next scene. Then all but three
people fall to their knees and take up positions
facing audience. Left standing are one* GI,
a MOTHER, *a* GIRL. *They are in the center of
the mass of bodies in a triangle facing out-
ward. The females who play "sweethearts"
throughout the play kneel in front of the* GIRL.
Women who play "mothers" throughout the

68

play kneel in front of MOTHER. *Boys kneel in front of* GI. *As the scene begins all the actors on the floor should flirt with the audience, using only their eyes. It should be the effect of group snapshots in which only the eyes move. However, the three principals are mobile. As the scene progresses the three may change places. The scene should end with them clustered together, arms and bodies closely intertwined, but their faces still toward audience.*)

GI: March 9, 1966, My Tho, Vietnam. Dear Mother . . . My dear baby Janet . . .

MOTHER: March 9, 1966, Kittitas City, Washington. My dearest beloved son . . .

GIRL: March 9, 1966, Kittitas City, Washington. Hi, darlin! Hi, honey! Hello, my lemon-drop kid! Boy, Eugene, am . . .

GI: Hi, Mom. I'm staying warm. The sun here's about two thousand degrees. My feet are still coal black from . . .

MOTHER: I wish I could be making you some chicken and dumplings. They called me from . . .

GIRL: I'm counting the days till your tour of duty is up. How's the sightseeing in the rice paddies?

MOTHER: . . . the Washington Chapter of American Mothers and told me I'd been chosen our state's Mother of the Year. O.K., now have a good laugh.

GI: . . . being wet and walking in the rice paddies, but on Sunday, I'm going to bleach them out with lemon like you suggested. Janet, baby, I can't stop thinking about that Goulet record. War is terrible, honey, but one thing it sure as hell teaches you is what it . . .

MOTHER: I guess I do feel proud, but I hate to think that one of the reasons they're making me Mother of the Year is because you are fighting for our country so far away on a foreign shore.

GIRL: . . . Boy, I know I'm supposed to cheer you up when I write you and all, but the television news scares you know what right out of me, honey. I know you have to fight for freedom, but honey, please don't go out of your way . . .

GI: . . . is that is important in life. And you are it for me. Mom, I'm so glad you're managing to keep busy and all.

MOTHER: . . . The farm is . . . doing fine, but I have to tell you I've had to lease out most of it. But I kept the piece of land where you rigged the swimming hole in the irrigation ditch . . .

GIRL: . . . I ache for you. I love your letters. I've got them all near memorized . . .

GI: You wouldn't believe how being tired and away from home and loved ones can knock you out. . . .

GIRL: By the time you get home, I just know I'll have

enough in savings for our down payment. Our house. Just us. . . .

MOTHER: I'd give my right arm, if I could just hear your voice on the phone. But I'm placing my trust in God, and in your good sense.

GI: Well, Mom, I have to hit the sack. . . .

GIRL: I got all the furniture all picked out for the master bedroom. . . .

MOTHER: Got to find something to wear when they pin that corsage on me. Hope it isn't gardenias. . . .

GI: Keep the letters coming, honey. They mean a lot. I'm putting on weight, Mom.

GIRL: I want you. I'll write you again before I go to bed. . . .

MOTHER: I love you with all my heart. . . .

GI: . . . Your loving son, Eugene. . . .

GIRL: Oh, Eugene, Eugene, my Eugene . . . Your own little girl, Janet. . . .

MOTHER: Come home just as soon as you can; all my love, dearest son, Your Mom.

GI: Stay by me, Janet. I'll be home soon. All my love, Eugene. . . .

> (*By now the three have locked arms in a circle and keep turning while saying their last sentences. This should repeat until all actors are standing. With the closing lines, all actors*

71

*should rise and march their counterpart to
the next formation. All girls go to back wall
or side wall to become male South Vietnamese
soldiers. The men march around stage to the
shouts of their* SERGEANT. *The girls assemble
themselves in an extraordinarily ragged and
unruly line. They are now South Vietnamese
soldiers. They make their lunches as they wait
in the hot sun. They entertain themselves by
singing sentimental love songs. Each actress
should sing her favorite secret love song. All
this should go on at the same time. One defi-
nitely should sing "Someone to Watch over
Me.")*

SERGEANT (*To men*): Halt! At ease, girlie burgers.
GI'S: You said it. We been on the steam table nine days
long.

SERGEANT (*Gesturing to girls*): Meet your comrades in
arms. These here are our allies and your
counterparts. The ARVN troops. These here
is the South Vietnamese men you're going
to teach to fight like American soldiers.

GI's: They're awful little.

SERGEANT: But big enough to pull a trigger.

GI ONE: They's so purty, they look like girls.

SERGEANT: These is your new buddies. You are here
to train them to be like you.

GI Two: I don't trust girls.

SERGEANT: These are South Vietnamese troops. And *you* are girls.

GI THREE: But, but, Sergeant . . .

SERGEANT: Dry up, Esmeralda!

GI FOUR: They ain't big enough to carry a gun.

SERGEANT: You'll teach 'em. They'll learn to shoot, but just be sure the guns ain't pointed at you.

GI's (*Laughing*): Get him. Gee whiz, Sarge, you're always joking us.

SERGEANT: You keep your eyes swiveled.

GI FIVE: Sergeant, what do the Viet Cong look like?

SERGEANT (*pointing to girls*): Like them.

GI SIX: How do we know who to shoot at?

SERGEANT: You shoot by ear, boobie. If you hear someone shoot at you, you shoot back.

GI's: Yes, sir.

SERGEANT: You better believe it! Live by your ears, Alice, and you might grow up to be Elizabeth.

GI THREE: You said *I* was Elizabeth.

SERGEANT: That was yesterday. Today is today. And don't you forget it, Maude!

GI's (*Saluting*): Yes, siree . . . Mother . . .

SERGEANT: Now get out there and win those guys' hearts and win those guys' minds, or we'll never get those guys' trigger fingers on our guys' side.

73

GI SEVEN: Can they talk American? SERGEANT: teach 'em. What's the matter with you shitheads— are you ladies or are you girls?

GI's (*Shouting*): Ladies!

SERGEANT (*Yelling back*): Gung Ho—satchmo!

GI's (*Yelling back*): Right away!

> (*The* SERGEANT *stalks off. The* GI's *gingerly and shyly kick the dirt all the way to where the Vietnamese sit, eating and humming. They try to get their attention.*)

JERRY (*Taking the situation in hand*): Hi there! How ya doing? Way to go. Thata boy. What a' ya say?

ARVIN: I like you—you number one big shot of the world.

JERRY: Hey, that's pretty good. Ain't it, boys?

GI's: That's pretty good. But do they know any Rock?

JERRY (*Squatting by the girls*): Me Yankee.

ARVIN (*Repeating after him*): Me Yankee.

JERRY: Yeah, hey hey, that's pretty good. Ain't it, boys?

GI's: Yeah, pretty good. Way to go.

JERRY: Me Yankee, you dickhead.

ARVIN (*Repeating*): Me Yankee, you dickhead.

JERRY: Well now, that's pretty good, but it's (*he gestures to himself and then to them*) Me, Me,

Me, Jerry, Me Yankee, you, you, you South Vietnamese, you dickhead.

ARVIN (*Nodding happily*): Oooooooooooooooooooooo. We get. We dickhead, you Yankee.

JERRY (*Pleased with himself*): That's right, that's right. (*Points to his head*) Head. (*Arvin repeats in Oriental-French accent*) Nose, clothes, arms, hand. Finger. Trigger finger. (*They hold up trigger fingers.*)

GI's: Come on, Jerry. Ask them where the girls are.

JERRY: Shut up, you guys. Don'tcha know, there's a war on? (*Back to Arvin*) Boot. One boot. Two boot.

ARVIN (*Likes the sound of that. They start singing*): One boot. One boot. One boot loved two boot.

JERRY: That's good. That's good. Gee, these guys learn fast.

GI's: Yeah, but don't they know any Rock?

JERRY (*To* ARVIN): Only one thing, you cute little guys. One thing. Don't shoot the boot. No no no. Don't shoot the boot.

ARVIN: No no no. We no shoot the boot. Love boot.

JERRY: No shoot the boot boot. Shoot the head, or shoot heart heart. No shoot the boot boot. Shoot the heart.

ARVIN: No no no no shoot heart. Love in heart.

JERRY (*Getting mad*): Come on, you guys. There's a

war going on here. You got to shoot the enemy's heart. Come on, you guys.

ARVIN: Ooooooooooooooooooooooooo we get. No shoot the boot boot. Shoot the heart heart.

JERRY: That's right, way to go. Good show. Gee, these guys are pretty damn smart. Look how fast they learn. (*To his men.*) Hey, you guys, aren't these little guys smart?

GI's: Gee, they're smarter than we thought. Ask them where the girls are.

JERRY (*Gives his men a tough look. Back to* ARVIN): Gee, you guys are awfully cute. Maybe I'll take back one for Mom. You appeal to my American heart.

ARVIN: Shoot the heart heart.

JERRY: That's right, that's right, but not mine. The Viet Cong. The enemy. You know the enemy. We call him Victor Charlie, that's code. The other guy. You know, get out there and get that guy and shoot him in his heart heart. Me— I'm your Yankee teacher.

ARVIN: You bet your boot boot.

JERRY: Gee, you guys have a way of catching on.

GI's: Hey, Jerry, ask them where the girls are.

JERRY (*To men*): Get me an M-18! (*They do so.*) This is my big gun. (*He picks out a girl.*) This is your best friend. Hey, you, you there,

come out here. (*She comes out shyly.*) Hold
the gun. (*She does.*) Now, tell me about the
gun.

MURIEL: Boot.

JERRY: No no no boot. That is gun.

MURIEL: Gun.

JERRY: Yeah, gun. Tell me about it.

MURIEL (*Looks at her friends, they gesture to her*):
Gun. Gun heavy.

JERRY: That's right. What else?

MURIEL: Gun heavy. Gun greasy.

JERRY: That's right. What else?

(MURIEL *shrugs her shoulders.*)

JERRY: This gun is an instrument. What can you do with
this instrument?

MURIEL: This gun is heavy, greasy instrument. (*She
pauses, looks at her friends, then she goes into
wild Dixieland pose and puts the gun barrel
to her mouth as if it were a trumpet.*) And
. . . I'm a gonna blow it. . . . (*Fast chorus
of "The Saints Go Marching In," and her
friends join in. Chaos.*)

JERRY (*Restoring order*): Hey, you guys, ten-hut! Ten-
hut! (*He gestures to his comrades.*) Issue them
M-18's with fixed bayonets. Now you guys, follow me. Do what I do. Chop chop. Kill kill.
That's the way.

> GI's *go through attack-and-kill pantomime,*
> *while singing the following song)*:

JERRY: What's the spirit of the bayonet?

ROY: The spirit of the bayonet is . . .

GI's: Kill kill kill.

JERRY: The spirit of the bayonet?

ALL: Kill kill kill.

JERRY: Chop chop.

ROY: Kill kill.

JERRY: Warm blood chop.

ROY: Warm blood kill.

JERRY: The spirit of the bayonet?

ALL: Kill kill kill.

ROY: The spirit of the bayonet?

ALL: Kill kill kill.

> Chop chop
> Kill kill
> Chop chop
> Kill kill
> The spirit of the bayonet
> Chop spirit chop
> Kill blood kill
> Chop spirit chop

Kill blood kill
The spirit of the bayonet
Kill Kill Kill!

JERRY (*Addresses this to the audience*): Now, we're off on a war game. This is just pretend, see. We're going out to look for V-C. We're going to flush him out and then we're going to engage him, and then we're going to kill that guy. But this first time, it's just pretend, see? Pretend. (*He makes a shush with his finger and his eyes twinkle. Back to the troops.*) Now you new guys get in back of these seasoned troops here. (*He gestures to his men, who line up in front of the girls.*) O.K., everybody. All together now. Sound off! (*They count cadence. At shout of four, the* ARVIN *turn into Viet Cong and stab our boys in the back with the bayonets. The men fall. The gals pick over their bodies looking for weapons to steal. Then all but two run and hide.*)

SERGEANT (*Comes stalking on*): All right, you guys. Let's shape up to ship out. (*He stops cold when he sees the scene of destruction. His nose runs.*) What's this? What's this? My little girls. My boys, my men. What the shit happened to my men?

ARVIN (*Two girls are left. One of them pretends to be hurt. The other holds her. They look at him and say*): Sorry about that.

SERGEANT: It's all my fault. They was still wet behind the ears. I shouldn't've left 'em alone. Which way did the bastards go? V-C. You see V-C? (*The girls nod.*) Which way . . . which way? (*The girls point in all directions.*)

SERGEANT: I'll get me a bag of new recruits. I'll run down them V-C's and rub their noses in it. (*Addressing the audience*) I wish the people back home could see this sight. They wouldn't have any question any more of why we is here. Look at my ladies. I nursed 'em through boot and stopped the airsickness. I taught them how to kill. You're never ready for death. Never. I seen it over and over. Young men, never ready for death. Not one is. Never. I would like to take every one of those bleeding-heart liberals and make him put each one of our dead boys in the green bag death sack. I would like to see those baldheaded, wet-mouthed liberals up to their balls in the blood of our boys and see how they could take loading these sweet lost bodies into the death-copter. I'd give both my arms for one sight like that. Those sons-of-bitching V-C are going to pay for the lives of my guys, even if I personally have to hunt down and skin each and every one of them. You'll see me again. You can bet your ass on that! (*The girls run off with their weapons and hide. The* SERGEANT *executes a complete about-face in place. He treats the fallen men as if they're sleeping in their sacks. He wakes them from a deep sleep.*) All right, boobies. Up and at 'em. Get the lead out. Get out of that sack. Ship up your shapes. I just lost my crack squad to the dirty sneaky charlies, and you're going out to get even with them if it's the last thing you ever do. And it may be. Get me? Wipe the snot off your nose, droopy drawers. Smarten up and fly right. You're going to shape up so fast you won't have time to shit.

GI's: Yes, sir. Yes, siree, Mother!

SERGEANT: Forward march.

(*The men march forward and walk square into the wall. They fall. Then they turn on their bellies and crawl across an open rice paddy as the mortars go off and sniper bullets zing by. One by one they raise their heads and address the audience.*)

GI ONE: When I was a little boy I used to eat a spoonful of dirt every day.

GI TWO: Similar things are not identical.

GI THREE: I seem to have a lot of ground to cover.

GI FOUR: Six per cent of the world's population controls sixty per cent of its wealth.

GI FIVE: Hello, young lovers.

GI SIX: Green Mint Formula 47 gives you confidence about your mouth.

GI Seven: When I get home I'm gonna run for Congress.

GI Eight: Have you been paid this week?

GI One: It's all right to be angry. It's all right.

GI Two: They laughed when I stood up to shoot.

GI Three: I thought you were going to phone me?

GI Four: Go down Moses, Jack, Jim, and Sally.

GI Five: I dreamed I saw J.F.K. last night alive as you and me.

GI Six: "Nothing is worth my life."

GI Seven: For the last seven years we've been sending children through college.

GI Eight: God love you.

GI One: You have the smile of an angel. An angel.

> (*A mortar explodes. They dive for cover.* Jerry *is hurt. He moans and screams. The men crawl to him and try to administer to his wounds. The* Sergeant *sends over his walkie-talkie for the helicopter. The men lift* Jerry *and move slowly in a circle as if in a helicopter. Then they place him alone on floor of stage. All go to the benches to be ready for the next scene.* Jerry *is alone lying on the stage; he pulls his shirt over his face. An actress steps forward and sings.*)

SINGER:

> Please God, I ask not for myself.
> Please God, bring him home safe.
> Please God, he has a heart of gold.
> Please God, watch over his life,
> He has only six more months to go.

> (*A family sits together on a bench to one side of the stage. An* OFFICER *appears and knocks.*)

OFFICER: Mr. Small?

FATHER: Yes?

OFFICER: I'm Captain Statzz. I'm to accompany your wife to Vietnam.

FATHER: Yes, of course. She'll be ready in a minute. (*He goes to his wife, and she shakes her head. They freeze.*)

SINGER (*Sings to Music of "Please God"*):

> His mother waits to see his face,
> To press the beat of his heart of gold.
> Please God, bring him home safe,
> Our family Marine with stance so bold,
> He has only six more months to go.

MOTHER: No. You go.

FATHER: Dear. You're the only one allowed.

MOTHER: I can't stand it.

FATHER: You've got to.

83

BROTHER: I'll go, Mother.

FATHER: You keep out of this.

SISTER: Don't talk to him that way.

FATHER (*Glares at child*): Sweetheart, I'll get your bag. The officer is waiting to escort you. This is Captain Statzz. My wife, Mrs. Small.

OFFICER: Jerry's mother?

MOTHER: Yes. (*They freeze.*)

SINGER (*Sings*):

> Please God, it's not too late.
> Please God, his family prays.
> Please God, his loved ones wait.
> Please God, he's only nineteen,
> He has only six more months to go.

> (CAPTAIN *turns and changes into* PILOT. MRS. SMALL *kisses her husband goodbye and follows* PILOT.)

OFFICER: This way, Mrs. Small. Fasten your seat belt.

MOTHER: Sir, why can't my husband go too? After all, he's Jerry's father.

OFFICER: We only have seats for mothers.

MOTHER: All the rest of these seats . . .?

OFFICER: Will be occupied by mothers.

> (*Plane takes off. The* MOTHER *holds a baby in her arms, reminiscent of one of the poses of the* MADONNA *in Act One.*)

SINGER (*Sings*):

> His mother longs to see his face,
> To press the beat of his heart of gold.
> Please God,
> Please God,
> Please God,
> He has only six more months to go.
>
> (SINGER *retires to the bench. Plane lands.*
> PILOT *changes into* DOCTOR. *They walk to*
> *entrance of field hospital.*)

MOTHER: Is he here?

OFFICER: Down this corridor, Mrs. Small.

MOTHER: Are you sure you've done . . .

DOCTOR: All we know how.

MOTHER: How long, Doctor, how long do I . . . does
he have?

DOCTOR: I'm sure you'll have at least two hours.

MOTHER: Doctor?

DOCTOR: Yes?

MOTHER: Will he know me?

DOCTOR: You're his mother.

MOTHER: I'm his mother.

DOCTOR: Your son is tagged.

MOTHER: Tagged?

DOCTOR: Name, rank, and serial number on a tag at his wrist.

MOTHER: Will I know him?

DOCTOR: His voice—you'll know his voice.

MOTHER: You'll go with me?

DOCTOR: Mrs. Small, I'd like to, but I have many boys to save.

MOTHER: I can't do it.

DOCTOR: Mrs. Small, we're sorry about this.

MOTHER: Please come with me.

DOCTOR: I'm needed.

MOTHER: I don't know where to start.

DOCTOR: He should be the third man in.

> (*She starts down the path of boys. She finds hers and bends to read the tag.*)

MOTHER: Gerald . . . Gerald Rogers Small, Sp. 2nd Class, Co. 107. Gerald Rogers Small. Gerald Rogers? Doctor . . . Doctor . . . It's a mistake. It's all a mistake . . . a grave mistake.

DOCTOR (*Running in*): Mrs. Small . . . please, men are . . .

MOTHER: The tag. Doctor, the tag . . .

DOCTOR: Let's see.

MOTHER: A mistake. This says Gerald Rogers Small.

DOCTOR: Yes?

MOTHER: You see, it's all a mistake. My son's middle name isn't Rogers, it's Robert. Gerald Robert Small. Robert. Robert!

DOCTOR: So it does.

JERRY (*Moaning*): Momma . . . charming Jerry . . . Momma . . . charming Jerry . . .

MOTHER (*A chill goes through her as she recognizes her son's voice*): Jerry . . .?

DOCTOR (*Quietly*): The typist made the error, Mrs. Small. Sorry about that. (*He leaves.*)

MOTHER: Jerry . . .

JERRY: Momma . . . Momma?
(JERRY *dies. The* MOTHER *mourns. Abrupt transformation into a Buddhist funeral. The sound becomes Vietnamese. The scene transforms immediately from that of the army field hospital to a Vietnamese hamlet. The American* MOTHER *becomes the Vietnamese* MOTHER, *and* JERRY *becomes her dead son. All the other actors participate as villagers and mourners. The Buddhist* PRIEST *rises and presides over the group. His shoulders are tense, his eyes half-closed, and his voice has many tones and slides. The speech should be on tape but also should be said by the actor, sometimes synchronized, sometimes a little ahead of the tape, sometimes a bit behind the tape, but ending in synchronization.*)

87

PRIEST (*Burning incense in containers in both hands, he waves the incense as he bends and weaves in a slow-motion dance at foot of the body*): Whatever spirits have come together here, either belonging to the earth or living in the air, let us worship the perfect Buddha, revered by gods and men; may there be salvation. Whatever spirits have come together here, either belonging to the earth or living in the air, let us worship the perfect Dharma, revered by gods and men; may there be salvation. Whatever spirits have come together here, either belonging to the earth or living in the air, let us worship the perfect Sangha, revered by gods and men; may there be salvation. (*He looks toward the body and directs the next lines to the body and also to the congregation. All mourn.*) A Buddha is the embodiment of Dharma, which is his real body. He is identified with all the constituents of the universe. This body is invisible and universal. All beings "live and move and have their being in it."

(*Brief mourning and crying, then a man rises and sings to audience.*)

SETH (*Rises in a spotlight to sing alone to the audience*):

Don't put all your eggs in one basket.
Baskets wear out and men die young.
Better to marry trees or elephants.
Men die young,
Some cities survive.

Go and pick yourself one
Because men die young, my dear,
Because men die young.

Don't put all your eggs in one basket.
Find several to keep
In reserve, my dear.
Men die young.

Since men are dying younger every year,
Be careful what you choose
Or you'll be alone the next twenty years,
Because men die young, my dear,
Because men die young.

You don't want to lose
The chance to cover your bets,
So love as much as you can, my dear,
Because men die young.

Try all available delicacies,
Don't concentrate on only one,
Because men die young, my dear,
Because men die young.

Some cities survive,
Go and pick yourself one,
Because men die young, my dear,
Because men die young.

(*As actors get into place for next scene, all the
women except the one who is to play* HANOI

HANNAH *rush out into the audience as spot-lights pick out various sections of the house. Each woman chooses a section and delivers the same speech.*)

WOMEN: This war is worms. This war is worms invaded by worms. This war is eating away at the boy flesh inside my belly. This war stinks. This war takes men away and pins back the man in me so he can't kick and scream, which is his God-given right. This war stinks. This war makes everybody more warlike than they are anyway. This war invades me and makes me hate myself. I hate you. I hate you. And you—I hate you! (*Quieter*) This war is wounds. This war is worms.

(*Women take their places on bench at back on stage. The men, led by* SERGEANT, *crawl in and dig in for a siege. Much sound of mortar and gunfire. Then sudden stillness. The men are dug in. There is a lull. It's dark. They semi-relax and listen. Each may react to* HANNAH's *lines according to his character. Some make fun of her archaic English terms. The audience should hear what they say. A crazy Chinese soap-opera organ plays under her speech. She sits in chair to one side of stage and reads from copy over mike.*)

HANOI HANNAH: Good evening, my little baby ball, Yankee imperialists. How goes our tiny battle today? This is your bosom buddy and wishful lover, Hanoi Hannah, bringing you the truth from around the world. I'm here to keep you warm for your sweetheart back home. Float to your lover on my voice. See her sweet body and the nape of her dear neck after you have nuzzled her in the back seat of your roadster. Feel her pulsating to your eager hands under her shift as you undress her on the back seat of your touring car. Feel her rush to meet your passion, guiding the most exciting part of you into the most exciting part of her. Smell the pungent love you share. Do you not savor that moment again as you lie in your imperialistic criminal foxholes? You who bring murderous destruction to a people who fight only for their own homes. Where is your sweetheart now, my dear little baby ball GI's? She is in the arms of a new man back home, while you fight here in a foreign land. She is in the back seat of a 1966 roadster, with somebody else. And now HE is removing her shift and plunging into your property. How does that make you feel, GI? Does that make you want to fight for what is yours? Do so, my little imperialistic lovers, but do so in your own back-yard. (*She plays a short Oriental version of "Back in Your Own Back Yard." Marching music softly under the next speech.*) It's me again, your Indo-China lover, Hanoi Hannah, back again for our educational talk, my tiny round-eyed GI. You must understand that everything is divisible—especially the colossus of the United States, especially the immoral giant

91

of U.S. imperialism. It will be and should be split up and defeated. The people of Asia, Africa, and Latin America can destroy the United States piece by piece, some striking at its head and others at its feet. . . . You are too spread out, my tiny GI's. You cannot be every place at once. You cannot be here in Vietnam and also guard your Stateside sweetheart and your Momma too. And what of your dollars, your Yankee dollars, tiny round-eyed GI? Who is making all those dollars, while you fight here in mud and are sucked by leeches and get only army pay? Everything is divisible, my tiny GI. Your head may be divided from your trunk, your arm from your shoulder, your heart from your head, your sex from your soul. Pull yourself together and confess to the world that you were wrong. Victory will go to the people of the world! It is inevitable. Long live the victory of the people's war! (*Soft music again for the next speech.*) This is your wishful lover and bosom buddy, Hanoi Hannah, saying, sweet dreams in your hole, but I wouldn't close an eye; you may never open it again, tiny round-eyed GI. Good night, my bad little boys. I'll be with you again this time tomorrow night without a shift on. . . . Sweet nightmare and . . . Aloha. . . . (*She plays a crazy lullaby by an Oriental jazz band.*)

(*The men battle the V-C for an instant. Silence again and one of the boys takes out his guitar. The men lie in a bomb crater and come in on* "But I'm too far from home.")

JERRY:

I want a chocolate soda.
I want a cracker jack.

I want a little baby
To scratch my aching back.
I want my little baby
To scratch my aching back.

But I'm too far from home (*men join in*).

I traveled hot and dusty
And sweated all my pores.
I traveled hot and dusty,
My feets all fulla sores.

I want my little baby
To scratch my aching back.

But I'm too far from home (*men join in*).

I beat me down a jungle
And shot myself a man.
I beat me down a jungle
And shot myself a man.

Gimme my little baby
To scratch my aching back.

But I'm too far from home (*men join in*).

I got my rocket-launcher.
I got my M-18.
I got my rainslick poncho.
Got my playboy magazine.
But I—

Want my little baby
To scratch my aching back.

But I'm too far from home (*men join in*).

(*All but two men crouch down and begin to crawl across stage as if moving through high grass.*)

JOE (*A* GI, *waves to audience alone at end of song*): Hi, folks. I want to tell you how proud I am to be able to be in direct contact with such fine and sunny-eyed supporters as you great American people. I need that support, and I tell you it feels good where it is most needed, in my head and hands and heart. I'll fight for you. I'll fight for you guys any day of the week. You're good people. The best!* (*The* SERGEANT *pulls him down.*)

FRED (*A* GI, *addresses the audience alone*): Sometimes you have to do things that you wouldn't ordinarily choose to do because you happen to be born in the greatest country in the world. What if I'd been born in the underside of an

* Cue for alternate scene (page 106).

African tree, the daughter of a Pygmy witch doctor? I'm proud to serve and to save the people at home from having to fight on their very own doorsteps. I'll stay halfway around the world to see that our commitments are kept so my mom can get her milk on our front porch every morning without my mom having to duck the bullets. No, sir! (*The* SERGEANT *pulls him to ground and he starts crawling.*)

ROY (*Crawling and alternately resting*): Next battle, next battle I'm gonna get up on the high ground and put a bullet through the back of the sergeant's neck.

PAUL (*Crawling and alternately resting*): I don't care. I don't give a shit. I don't care. I can't . . . nothing . . . big zero. . . .

ROY: If I can just get high enough, the bullet will come out at the base of his collar in front and they'll never know. . . .

PAUL: I wouldn't give a shit if the whole planet melted into lava and made red candy hearts across the universe. I don't care. I'm not even angry . . . I don't care.

ROY: I'll get up in a high Vietnamese tree and next contact with the enemy I'll get him in the back of the neck. And then I'll stay there.

SETH: Do you know where I can buy a greeting card for a guy who's been blown up by a mine?

SERGEANT: Ten-hut. You've earned it, ladies—three-day
leave in Saigon.

(*They march off singing*):

Let's get to Saigon
And blitz the bars.
We'll load up on booze
Till we see stars.

Gonna get me a slant-eye
In old Saigon.
She'll feed me booze
And I'll make her a son.

We'll shack up tight
In her hootchie-cootch
And love all night
To the goonie-gootch.

Let's get to Saigon
And blitz the bars.
We'll load up on booze
Till we see stars.

Till we see stars
In her hootchie-cootch
And love all night
To the goonie-gootch.

Till we see stars!
Till we see stars!
Till we see stars.
Till we see stars. . . .

(The stage is filled with dancing bodies and SAIGON SALLY *sings in her bar and leads the dance. Two others join her in song.)*:

* Anti-hero baby
Anti-hero baby
Anti-hero baby
Anti-hero baby.
Baby, baby,
Hero baby mine

Anti-hero baby
Anti-hero baby
Anti-hero baby
Anti-hero baby
Baby, baby,
Hero baby mine

Anti-hero baby
Anti-hero baby
Anti-hero baby
Anti-hero baby
Baby, baby,
Hero baby mine

Anti-hero baby
Anti-hero baby
Anti-hero baby
Anti-hero baby
Baby, baby,
Hero baby mine

* Pick up here at end of alternate scene (p. 110).

Anti-hero baby
Anti-hero baby
Anti-hero baby
Anti-hero baby
Baby, baby,
Hero baby mine

Anti-hero baby
Anti-hero baby
Anti-hero baby
Anti-hero baby
Baby, baby,
Hero baby mine

(*As the dance ends an exuberant* GI *shouts a toast. The* SERGEANT *drinks at the bar. Couples pair off and slower dancing begins.*)

GI: Here's to Saigon Sally! She runs the swingingest bar in all Vietnam!

SALLY: Sure I do, baby. You and me and LBJ.

GI (*Toasting*): Barbecue today with LBJ. (*As the toast sinks in the* SERGEANT'S *clouded brain, he begins to smolder. He whips around and tries to see which one of his men is shouting.*)

GI: Let's all go gay for LBJ.

GI: I lost my way with LBJ.

GI: March to doomsday with LBJ.

GI: I lost my green beret on the Road to Mandalay.

ALL (*Singing*): Glory, Glory, what a hell of a way to die.

GI: I got syphillis today, courtesy LBJ.

ALL (*Singing*): Glory, Glory, what a hell of a way to die! . . . And we never shot a goddam Cong!

SERGEANT (*Bulldozing his way into the men and breaking them up*): Knock it off, you boozed-up pussies! Knock it off!

GI (*Still carried away*): Moral decay with LBJ!

SERGEANT (*Shoving him*): Knock it off, you traitor. You're talking about my President. I love my President. (*Talking at the* GI) I love our President. If this guy would talk like I know he can talk instead of all this peace, hope and stop and end war talk, I just know he could put them all down. We're not much more than fleas—so why don't we talk like fleas? Why doesn't this guy talk to them like I know he could? All his speech writers get in between him and us. Our peace Pope! Pope Pipe! I mean if our President can scratch his balls in public and those fancy pants in London don't like it, I say we learned it from them. They ain't so far up since Shakespeare! (GI *he's been haranguing pushes him away gently and points him toward another couple.*)

GI: Tell them. Tell them.

SERGEANT (*Weaving over to the next couple*): I think this guy is really in touch with the people.

(*All the actors stop dancing in couples and begin to become aspect of the* SERGEANT'S *nightmare. They alternately accuse and attack him with images that have occurred throughout the play—drill, salutes, pushups, bayonetting, the Madonna, Jerry's death, Vietnamese mothers. The scene should become phantasmagoric.*) He knows what's happening. But the Eastern King Makers got their prejudice out for him! Poor bastard, it's more important that he should cut his nails right than he should make peace in the world. (*He collars another couple.*) Right now we're in the grips of the most prejudiced war we've ever fought. The Jews are mad that we're finally fighting for a minority *before* the genocide; they don't want no fights unless it's for them. This here minority ain't Western European; they's our little yellow-skinned brothers with slant eyes and too small to tote our guns. They think it's more important that that guy in the White House learn to eat lung under glass. I say warm yer spareribs! (*He starts to chant.*) Get on with the war! (Everyone *picks it up and chants "Get on with the war." They chant and dance to a terrific pitch, then silence.*) Get on with this war—and—win it! I say take it out. Take it out and let's see how long it is against Mao Tse! Take it out! Take it out! Remove it! I love our President. I love our President. (*To* SAIGON SALLY) I love our President!

SALLY (*Trying to calm him. He collapses into her arms*):
Sure you do, baby.

GI: Sing us another song, Sal.

SALLY: Sure I will, baby. (*Embracing* SERGEANT) Come
on, baby. You had yourself quite a blow.

GI: Come on and sing us another one, Sal.

SALLY (*Pulling the clumsy* SERGEANT *to her and talking
directly to him*): Sure I will, baby. Dance with
me? (*As she sings, the other couples dance
slowly and lovingly.*)

Close your eyes and dance awhile,
Close your eyes and kiss my neck,
Just relax, you'll get the hang,
Close your eyes and kiss my chin,
Honey, relax, put down that gin.

Close your eyes and dance awhile,
Close your eyes and kiss my neck,
Just relax, you'll get the hang,
Close your eyes and kiss my chin,
Honey, relax, put down that gin.

Close your eyes and dance awhile,
Dance awhile, dance awhile,
Close your eyes and dance awhile,
Dance awhile, dance awhile.
That's the way,
That's the style,
Close your eyes and dance awhile,
Now, kiss my chin.

(Giant explosion. The bar is blown to bits. The explosion reverberates and repeats. As it begins to die down we see all the bodies exploding to the pulse of the sound. This is done in slow motion. As the sound dies away we see everyone in a clustered death struggle. The bodies are massed together center stage, tangled and flailing in slow motion. They stab one another, shoot one another, and choke one another as they fall in a heap to the floor. All sound has stopped. There is no sound of the death struggle. When all are dead they are in a tangled circle on the floor, the reverse of the beautiful circle of the opening image. There is silence for the count of ten. Then flat, emotionless voices are heard saying the following lines. The lines must not be said with any personal attitude and should overlap. The director should assign the lines to the actors.)

Doves. War. Take away. Treasure lost. Lost our treasure. Lose our treasure. Spend all our natural resources. Cannon fodder. The cost is high. And our boys our dollars. Dollars beget dollars but boys don't come back. My boy, my boy. Come back. Bring him back. Bring back my boy. Dear God. Dear God. Hear me you bloody blessed and deadening God. Hear me dear God. Hear my prayer dearest God. I will give all my dollars to bring my boy back home again. All my dollars. Let him come home again. I

give all.   All all all my dollars.   I give all my
dollars.   Let him come home once again.
Blow it up.   Blow it.   Blow the whites of his
frigging eyes to kingdom come again.   Blow
the rice right out of his gut.   Gut his gut.
Gut to gut.   Butt to butt.   Crack his nuts.
Destroy his blood.   Spill blood.   Show your
love by spilling your blood.   The death ship.
Grenade.   Blow.   Bullet.   Bayonet.   Knife.
Cut.   Slash open his neck or lay down yours.
Move it shithead.   Get the lead out dickhead.
Come on girls lift up your skirts and wiggle
your way to glory.   Wiggle your way.   Wiggle
your ass.   Fart that gas and putt your butt to
glory.   Bug out you scab.   Bug out.
Bugged.   Buggest.   Bugged.   A point of no
return.   No return.   A point.   There is a
point somewhere.   There is a point where all
the points jab the head of the angel.   Super
super sonic blades.   Travel super.   Argue
freedom.   Happy days honey.   Up yours
bunny.   Funny you used to be so sunny.   I
fought for you upstairs.   Loony tunes.   Hi ya
doc! Humphrey's voyage of reassurance.   But
Gandhi's dead.   Chocolate soda.   Two
scoops.   Big Daddy Flew Out.   To give us a
handout.   Out.   Out.   Oops there goes my
arm again.   There goes my head again.
Shooting through the Blue Yonder my boys.
Oops there went the green of my eyes and the
glow of my heart.   Oops there went my belly
into the gully.   Remember me to Mom boys.

And have another shave. When you get back
think of me boys. Think of me. Oops there
went my legs again. The sun also rises but not
my cock. Goodbye to the thunder of the Sun.
You son-of-a-bitch. Goodbye dickheads of
the world. Who needs me. Who needs this.
Who needs war. Who needs this shit. I'm in
the shit. Who needs me. Who. Who needs.
Who needs. Who.

(*Then the entire company says the following
together and the heap should pulse like a giant
beating heart.*)

WHO   WHO   WHO
WHO   WHO   WHO
WHO   WHO   WHO
WHO————!

(*As the last line dies away there is silence for
a count of twenty. Then one by one the actors
rise. They must do so in extremely slow motion as if coming back from a long distance.
They are fragile. They are angels. They are
beautiful. One by one they stand. One by one
they enter the audience. Each chooses an audience member and touches his hand, head,
face, hair. Look and touch. Look and touch.
A celebration of presence. They go among the
audience until every actor has left the stage.
Then as the song begins they leave the audi-
torium. In no way should the actors communicate superiority. They must communicate the*

wonder and gift of being actually alive to-
gether with the audience at that moment.

Far across the Southern Sea
Is a land where Viets rock.
Here every morning you can see
The Viets roll.

When the bombs fall
The Viets rock and rock,
When the napalm bursts
Then the Viets roll.

At the sound of jets
The Viets rock and rock,
When the tracers flash
Then the Viets roll.

Rock and roll, rock and roll.
How the sweet Viets
Love to rock and roll.
Those dear little Viets
Love our rock and roll.

Do the Viet Rock,
Watch that Viet roll,
Do the Viet Rock,
Watch that Viet roll.
That's the way the Viets rock,
All the way the Viets roll,
Rock and roll, rock and roll,
Do the Viet Rock.

CURTAIN

ALTERNATE SCENE TO BE USED IN PLACE OF OR IN ADDITION TO FINAL CRAWLING SCENE

> (*Begin after* JOE's *speech, page 94. Cue:* JOE: . . . *I'll fight for you guys any day of the week. You're good people. The best!*)

> (*Abrupt transition. All actors are now V-C. A Viet Cong stronghold. A local tribunal is present. It is presided over by the local V-C* COMMANDER. *At his side sits his beautiful Vietnamese* MISTRESS. *The* COMMANDER *reaches over and squeezes his mistress's breast. She pretends to sigh. But her eyes are apprehensive. He pulls her to him and leans on her voluptuously. He turns and calls to a guard.*)

COMMANDER: Bring in the Uncle Sam criminal.

SOLDIER (*Speaking Oriental gibberish, pushes in one of our GI's. He's tied to a stake at his back; there is Oriental writing on the stake. It isn't a stationary stake, but runs only down as far as his hips.*)

COMMANDER: Good morning, barbarian mafia. It is time for you to leave our lovely world. Do you have anything to say before you depart?

GI (*Looks briefly at girl and we see something flash between them*): Allen, Seth, Private First Class, 113345679GHT, U.S. Army.

COMMANDER: I repeat, this is your last sunrise. You are to die for the blood of our heroic brother that was shed in Saigon this time yesterday morning. A wanton murder by criminal puppets of the Jesse James, U.S. Uncle Sam imperialist invaders. Is there nothing you want left hanging on our air waves?

GI (*Bravely*): Allen, Seth, Private First Class, 113345679GHT, U.S. Army.

COMMANDER: Billy Barbarian the Kid Machine! (*He spits at GI, then kisses and fondles his mistress and looks to see the effect on the soldier.*) Are you sure there isn't something you'd like to whisper. A sweet nightingale song, perhaps, into a lotus ear?

GI: Allen, Seth, Private First Class, 113345679GHT, U.S. Army.

COMMANDER (*Looks at his watch*): I've indulged you enough, Ma Rainey vicious mad-dog-killer of trees and huts. Parade the criminal.

(Two V-C *parade the* GI *around the village, dragging and kicking him. Villagers throw dirt and spit on him. One demented villager almost foams at the mouth while punching and scratching at the* GI, *babbling in gibberish and getting more and more excited. As the violence mounts, the* MISTRESS *of the* COMMANDER *begins to perspire and inadvertently clutches the arm of her master. He notices it.*)

COMMANDER: Stop! (*He gestures toward the excited, demented* V-C.) Come. (*To* GI) His entire family was burned before his eyes from your napalm Baby Face Nelson. Come, little one. (*To demented* V-C.) You can have revenge. Which part of this pig do you want to hang from a pole outside your cave? Take your time, choose with care. Only one piece. There isn't enough of this skinny Capone to go around. (*The* V-C, *nearly drooling with glee, looks all over the* GI. *First he grabs a thumb, then an ear, a nose, his tongue. He shakes his head, finally points to* GI's *chest where his heart would be.*) Heart? (*The* MISTRESS *lets a little cry escape her. The* COMMANDER *turns and grabs her and twists her arm.*) Now I know where you've been stealing when the moon is high. If you've lifted your slippers heavenward for him you can now share his fate. (*He pushes her out into the clearing and she bumps into* SETH. *He tries to show no emotion but is clearly distressed.*) Now she's close enough for you to whisper into her traitorous ear.

GI: You're unjust.

COMMANDER: Don't tell me what I am, Legs Diamond. (*He carefully aims at the girl.*) Kneel.

MISTRESS (*Kneeling*): Yes, my lord.

COMMANDER: Put your head to the earth of your ancestors.

MISTRESS (*Touching ground with her head*): Yes, my lord.

COMMANDER (*Watching* GI *all the time, he walks slowly*

to the girl and puts the barrel of the gun against the back of her neck. To SETH): Is there something you wanted to say now?

GI: You're making a mistake.

COMMANDER: It is you who have made the mistake. (*He fires his gun into the girl's head and she falls at the feet of the* GI. *He flinches and tries not to gasp.*) It is your turn. You have one more chance to give information to save your corrupt skin.

GI: Allen, Seth, Private First Class . . .

COMMANDER: Little one. Would you like the honor? (*He brings the demented* V-C *to his side.*) Come, I'll help you hold the gun. We'll shoot him bit by bit. (*The little one, foaming and gurgling, leaps to the* COMMANDER. *Together they get the gun pointed at* SETH.) First his belly. (*Bang.*) Good. Good. Now, a shot for each shoulder. (*Bang, bang.*) Excellent. Now his pee pee. (*Bang.*) Good.

GI (*Listing, but still trying to stand tall*): Allen, Seth, Private First Class . . .

COMMANDER: No, no, little one. Don't aim for the heart. That's for your very own. The nose. No. The eyes? One for each of those ugly round Yankee eyes. Two for you, round eyes. (*Bang, bang.*)

V-C (*Jumps up and down with glee and runs to body and begins to chop at the chest and pulls out*

the heart and sucks on the stringy arteries):
Ummmmmmm ymmmmmmmm. . . .

COMMANDER: Mine their bodies with grenade booby
traps. Leave them on the trail for the next GI
platoon to stumble over. (*He grabs another
woman and fondles and kisses her and says
sweet things in gibberish while bodies are
rigged and light fades.*)

(*Song: "Men Die Young," to be placed here
instead of after Buddhist funeral.*)*

* Continue on page 97.

COMINGS AND GOINGS

◼

A Theatre Game

◼

For The Firehouse Theatre Company,
Minneapolis, Minnesota

PRODUCTION NOTES

■

This play is meant for both actors and audience to be an enjoyment of technique—pure virtuosity on the part of the actors. The fun of the play is in how much and how involved the audience gets. When we did it at Café La Mama Experimental Theatre Club, some people came three nights in a row to see it. It was never the same play. I've thought since that we should have done it twice in one night. The play taxes not only the actor's imagination, but his physical prowess, team ability, and intellect.

It can be approached in two ways, and I know an imaginative director will find others. We played it with a small card on which all the actors' names were printed. A wheel was spun by a disinterested party at intervals of thirty-five to ninety seconds. A name was called out and one actor ran into the play and another actor ran out.

I had originally thought the director would sit on one of the benches with the actors and send them in as a coach does at a basketball game, and I'd still like to try this. However, it might take away from some of the marvelous chance comedy that resulted from one personality taking over a role begun by a quite different personality—sometimes in mid-sentence.

We staged the play in the center of the café, with a small bench for the men on one side and another for the women on the opposite side. The person who spun and called sat in full view of the audience and behaved with the attitude of an official at a tennis match or basketball game. The women were dressed in tights and simple free-flowing colorful dresses. The men wore white ducks and brilliant hockey jerseys. There were three small white boxes and one white platform for them to work with. The platform at times doubled as a throne, a sailing ship, and an Indian pony. The resourcefulness of the players seemed boundless and grew with every performance.

Besides being great fun to watch and do, the play can train the actor in concentration, focus, flexibility, and ensemble work. The words are there and in a firm enough situation so that the main equipment of the actor is free to fly once the technical part of the play is under his belt. I like to think of the play as a trampoline for actors and director. We played with three men and three women. But more or fewer would work. It could even be done as a straight transformation play with one man and one woman. The director should feel free to cut any scene he and the actors can't solve.

COMINGS AND GOINGS

■

A Theatre Game

> (*A man and a woman rise from a bench, walk to stage center, and settle themselves.* SHE *curls up, more asleep than awake.*)

HE (*Alert and threatening*): Touch me.

SHE: In a minute.

HE: Now.

SHE: In a minute.

HE: It's morning.

SHE: In a minute.

HE: It's time.

SHE: In a minute.

HE: I'm leaving.

SHE: In a minute.

HE: Touch me.

SHE: In a minute

HE: I'm leaving now.

SHE: In a minute.

HE: Goodbye.

SHE: No.

HE: Yes.

SHE: In a minute.

HE: Minute's up.

SHE: No.

HE: Now.

SHE (*Getting up*): O.K.

> (*Repeat this scene three times. All the scenes are to be transformed one into the other without pause.*)
>
> (*A kitchen*)

SHE: Put down that gun and help me with these dishes.

HE: I'm not finished cleaning it.

SHE: You're always cleaning that dangerous weapon in my clean kitchen.

HE: Where else should I clean it? Where else? You set me such a good example of how to clean a kitchen I naturally think it's the best place to clean the damn gun.

SHE: Don't you dare swear in my clean kitchen.

HE: You just swore in your clean kitchen.

SHE: I never did no such thing.

HE: Double negative, double negative.

SHE (*Washing dishes*): You can be so aggravating. God!

HE: There you did it again.

SHE: You don't give me a moment's peace.

HE: But that's all I want from you. (*He pats her fanny.*)

SHE (*Slapping him with the dishcloth*): Stop that, you dirty old man.

HE: I am *your* dirty old man. Your very own, very dirty old man. Come here. You want to clean me? Come on and clean me good. (*He hugs her and she responds, laughing.*)

(*In their clinch they change to a faulty plug in a wall socket.*)

SHE: What's wrong? I feel you've slipped.

HE: It's my left prong. The screw hole's stripped, I think.

SHE: Your lamp's blinking.

HE: I know. I know. The whole thing will blow out if that jerk don't put down his newspaper and screw it back in.

SHE: Not him again. He's so inept.

HE: She's better.

SHE: She can hold a wratchet at least.

HE: Can you give me more juice?

SHE: Don't be unintelligent.

HE: Can't you do something?

SHE: I can be constant, that's something.

> (HE *starts to shake her.* HE'S *pulling her out of a car. It's raining and they're on a curve of the highway at night.*)

HE: You stupid woman driver, do you know what you've done to my car? You shouldn't be driving. What are you—drunk or something? The curse? What excuse can you give me, can you give God? Do you know what's under that crushed door in the suicide seat of my car? We were taking a ride in the rain. My mother likes rain. I'm going to make you see her. I'm going to make you look at her. By the time I get through with you, you'll be behind bars for the next ninety years. (HE *opens her car door, still holding on to one of her shoulders, and drags the terrified woman from behind the wheel.* SHE'S *numb and in a state of shock.*)

SHE: It's raining. It's dark. It's raining.

HE: It's raining. It's beautiful. Why didn't you open your eyes? Do you have a license? I bet you don't have a license. How could you be allowed to drive? I wasn't going more than thirty-five. (*He pulls her close.*) Ahhhhrg, you've been drinking! Disgusting. It's too much.

SHE: It's my birthday. It's raining.

HE (*Propelling woman toward his car, he forces her head down to look at mangled body of his mother*): There! That's what you've done, you—you—you miserable!

SHE: Oh my God! Oh my God! She's still holding on to her purse. She's holding on to her purse like a little girl. She's still holding on.

HE (*Pulling her around*): I'm going to make you know what it feels like to have your face crushed in. (*He forces her down onto the road and is about to jump on her head.*)

(HE *becomes a pencil writing a list.* SHE *is the list and says the list as* HE *writes it with his body.*)

SHE: Take car to be greased.
      Pick up shirts.
      Check on George.
      Go to Joe's workshop.
      Plan the next five years.
      Get new underpants.
      Mail letters on way home.
      Stop at Roger's to get the key.
      Check on Mozart Masses.
      Attend Mr. Jordan's funeral.
      Take car to be greased. (HE *topples over to land beside her.*)

(*In bed in early morning*)

SHE: Honey?

119

HE: Arhgghhhh.

SHE: Alarm.

HE: Grrrrrrr.

SHE: Get up.

HE: Uhhhhhhhhhhhh.

SHE: Get up.

HE: Ghhhhhh.

SHE: Get up.

HE: Fuck it.

SHE: Not now.

HE: Arghhhhh.

SHE: Honey?

HE: O.K.

SHE: Honey?

HE: O.K.

SHE: Alarm.

HE: O.K.

SHE: Get up.

HE: O.K.

SHE: Honey?

HE: O.K. . . . (HE *leaps straight up in the air.*)

(*A living room.* HE *paces,* SHE *sits.*)

HE: I don't know why you expect so much. What more do you want? What else can I do? I'm here. I'm here with you. What else can I do that I'm not doing? What is it? I can't make it out. You don't tell me, yet—you want. You want. I can feel you crouched there inside that mound of you. And I know you want. But I don't know what it is that you want. What is it? Do you want it? Do you? You don't know what it is I'm talking about, do you? You don't—do you? And yet you sit there and you want. You want, you want. And I stand here, and I don't know what it is that you want, you want. I stand here, don't I? At least I'm here. I'm here with you. Look? See? Your man is here. Right here, see? Two arms, two legs, only one head, just like everybody else. Yet, you want. I feel that tug in you. Where do you want me? What do you want of me? Backward and forward, you want!

(SHE *cries.*)

HE: That's what you wanted? That's what you wanted? That's all you wanted. Cry? That's too easy. You can't get out of it that way. It's another trick to get me off the track. I'm going to find out if it takes me the rest of my life. I'm going to find out what it is you want. Do you hear me? I'm going to find out if it takes me the rest of my life. . . . The rest of my life! (SHE *begins to smile a tiny smile to herself.*)

121

> (SHE *rises to face him. Their bodies and faces take on Kabuki-like attitudes. The banal lines should be intoned with whining but amplified sounds as if calling to the dead.*)

HE: Where are you going?

SHE: To wee-wee.

HE: Good girl. When will you be back?

SHE: When I finish.

HE: Good girl. Bring me a cigarette.

SHE: In a minute.

> (*They change exact positions.*)

SHE: Where are you going?

HE: Bowling with the boys.

SHE: Good boy. When will you be back?

HE: When I finish.

SHE: Good boy. Bring me a cigarette.

HE: In a minute.

> (*Repeat above scenes three times. Then they relax into postures of American Indians in a cave.*)

HE: Morning Star?

> (SHE *smiles weakly.*)

HE: Mine.

SHE: Hot.

HE: Morning Star. (*Caresses her face.*)

SHE: Cold.

HE: Morning Star. (*Strokes her hair.*)

SHE: Hot.

HE: Food?

> (SHE *shakes her head.*)

HE: Love?

> (SHE *nods.*)

HE: Morning Star. (HE *sits near her and puts his blanket around them both.*)

SHE: Hot.

HE: Mine.

> (*A diner—* HE *orders breakfast. Matter-of-fact.* SHE'S *the waitress, casual.*)

HE: Orange juice.

SHE: Yes.

HE: Squeeze yourself?

SHE: Yes.

HE: Two fried eggs.

SHE: Yes.

HE: Sunnyside up.

SHE: Yes.

HE: Bacon.

SHE: Yes.

HE: Three pieces.

SHE: Yes.

HE: Not too well done.

SHE: Yes.

HE: Toast.

SHE: Yes.

HE: Two pieces.

SHE: Yes.

HE: Buttered.

SHE: Yes.

HE: Hash browns.

SHE: Yes.

HE: With onion.

SHE: Yes.

HE: Coffee.

SHE: Yes.

HE: Dark.

SHE: Yes.

HE: Water.

SHE: No.

> (*Breakfast at the diner. Master—slave. Waitress is master.*)

SHE: Orange juice.

HE: Yes.

SHE: Squeezed.

HE: Yes.

SHE: Two fried eggs.

HE: Yes.

SHE: Sunnyside up.

HE: Yes.

SHE: Bacon.

HE: Yes.

SHE: Three pieces.

HE: Yes.

SHE: Not too well done.

HE: Yes.

SHE: Toast.

HE: Yes.

SHE: Two pieces.

HE: Yes.

SHE: Buttered.

HE: Yes.

SHE: Hash browns.

HE: Yes.

SHE: With onion.

HE: Yes.

SHE: Coffee.

HE: Yes.

SHE: Dark.

HE: Yes.

SHE: Water.

HE: No.

> (*Breakfast at the diner. Master—slave. Customer is master.*)

HE: Orange juice.

SHE: Yes.

HE: Squeeze yourself?

SHE: Yes.

HE: Two fried eggs.

SHE: Yes.

HE: Sunnyside up.

SHE: Yes.

HE: Bacon.

SHE: Yes.

HE: Three pieces.

SHE: Yes.

HE: Not too well done.

SHE: Yes.

HE: Toast.

SHE: Yes.

HE: Two pieces.

SHE: Yes.

HE: Buttered.

SHE: Yes.

HE: Hash browns.

SHE: Yes.

HE: With onion.

SHE: Yes.

HE: Coffee.

SHE: Yes.

HE: Dark.

SHE: Yes.

HE: Water.

SHE: No.

> (*Breakfast at the diner—Automation. Both behave like pre-programmed robots. Square gestures, equal space beween words, and perfectly equal time between question and response.*)

SHE: Orange juice.

HE: Yes. Squeeze yourself?

SHE: Yes. Two fried eggs.

HE: Yes.

SHE: Sunnyside up.

HE: Yes. Bacon.

SHE: Yes. Three pieces.

HE: Yes. Not too well done.

SHE: Yes. Toast.

HE: Yes. Two pieces.

SHE: Yes. Buttered.

HE: Yes. Hash browns.

SHE: Yes. With onion.

HE: Yes. Coffee.

SHE: Yes. Dark.

HE: Yes. Water.

SHE: No.

> (*Breakfast at the diner—Bliss. Customer and waitress have symbiotic ecstatic relationship. Played with quiet warmth and secure joy.*)

HE: Orange juice.

SHE: Yes.

HE: Squeeze yourself?

SHE: Yes.

HE: Two fried eggs.

SHE: Yes.

HE: Sunnyside up.

SHE: Yes.

HE: Bacon.

SHE: Yes.

HE: Three pieces.

SHE: Yes.

HE: Not too well done.

SHE: Yes.

HE: Toast.

SHE: Yes.

HE: Two pieces.

SHE: Yes.

HE: Buttered.

SHE: Yes.

HE: Hash browns.

SHE: Yes.

HE: With onion.

SHE: Yes.

HE: Coffee.

SHE: Yes.

HE: Dark.

SHE: Yes.

HE: Water.

SHE: No.

(HE *leans on her as they struggle forward.*)

HE: We've walked miles.

SHE: Only a bit more.

HE: Give me some water.

SHE: We're out.

HE: I can't move.

SHE: Yes. Only a little way yet.

HE: Leave me here.

SHE: No.

HE: My stomach aches.

SHE: It'll stop.

HE: Farther?

SHE: Only a bit.

HE: Can you see?

SHE: Yes.

HE: How much?

SHE: Enough. There, just there, a little beyond.

HE: Thirsty.

SHE: Me too.

HE: Kiss?

SHE: One. (*A brief kiss.*)

HE: How much farther?

SHE: Only a bit. (*They fall asleep standing in place.*)

(*Waking up, still standing in place.*)

SHE: Honey . . .

HE: Mmmmmmmmmmmm.

SHE: Love you . . .

HE: Good girl . . .

SHE: Really love you . . .

HE: My doll . . .

SHE: Honey?

HE: I'm here.

SHE: I hate you to leave me.

HE: Is it the alarm?

SHE: Sorry, darling.

HE: Not your fault.

SHE: Angel, hold me one more time.

HE: One more time.

SHE: One more time.

HE: One more time.

SHE: Till tomorrow morning.

HE: Till tonight.

SHE: Lover?

HE: Tonight.

SHE: Tonight?

HE: You better believe it.

SHE: Bye bye, baby . . .

HE: Honey?

SHE: Now.

> (*They assume a Kabuki posture and* SHE *starts to move away from him.*)

HE: (*Kabuki voice*): Where are you going?

SHE: (*Kabuki voice*): To wash the clothes.

HE: Good girl. When will you be back?

SHE: When I finish.

HE: Good girl. Bring me a cigarette.

SHE: In a minute.

> (*They walk toward each other and collide. They pick each other up, threaten with arms and feet, then turn and walk away.*)

SHE: Where are you going?

HE: Crazy, wanna come along?

SHE: Good boy. When will you be back?

HE: When I finish.

SHE: Good boy. Bring me a cigarette.

HE: In a minute.

> (*They change exact physical places and stances with one another, asking each other casually,* "Where are you going? Where are you going?" *Then they intone:* "Crazy wanna come along? Crazy, wanna come along?")

> (*A kitchen.*)

SHE (*Her back to him*): I know you're here.

> (HE *smiles.*)

SHE: I know you're here.

> (HE *approaches.*)

SHE: My back's shivering.

> (HE *smiles.*)

SHE: I feel lighter. I know you're here.

HE: I've been gone a long time.

SHE: It doesn't matter.

HE: You've waited?

SHE: What else?

> (*He smiles.*)

SHE: You're here. All of you. You're here.

HE (*Embracing her*): We're here.

SHE: Let me turn away again.

HE: Why?

SHE: I want you all around me.

HE: Like this? (*Encircles her from behind.*)

SHE: Oh yes. Yes. Yes. Just like this. Yes.

> (HE *picks her up and holds her aloft.* HE *puts her down and smiles.* SHE *picks him up, holds him aloft, then drops him.* HE *falls and stays on the floor.*)

HE (*The rich man, Luke 16: 19. In hell in torment*): Father Abraham, have mercy upon me. Send Lazarus to dip the tip of his finger in water to cool my tongue; for I am tormented in this flame.

SHE (*as God*): Son, remember that you in your lifetime received your purple and fine linen and fared sumptuously every day: and Lazarus a beggar was laid at your gate full of sores. He asked only to be fed with the crumbs which fell from your table; moreover, you fed him not, but moreover, your dogs came and licked his sores, but now he is comforted here (*heaven*), and thou art tormented. And besides all this and moreover, between us and you a great chasm has been fixed, in order, moreover, that those who would pass from here to you may not be able to, and none may cross from there to us.

HE: I pray thee therefore, father, that thou wouldst send him to my father's house. For I have five brethren; so that he may testify unto them, lest they also come into this place of torment.

SHE: They have Moses and the prophets; let them hear them.

HE: Nay, father Abraham; but if some one went unto them from the dead they will repent.

SHE: If they hear not Moses and the prophets, neither will they be persuaded even though some one has risen from the dead.

(They rise and raise their hands above their heads. They study their hands. They lower their hands and look at them. They fit their hands one into the other. They look at each other. They pull their hands apart and the man and woman lace their hands together. They look down at their interwoven hands. They look into each other's eyes. Still with hands locked, HE leads her to a chair and seats her. Then their hands break apart. HE pats her shoulder.)

(We are now in a police station.)

HE: There now. Pull yourself together. It isn't as bad as all that. Stop crying, for God's sake. I'll just phone your husband, and we'll try to get this straightened out.

SHE *(Alarmed at word husband)*: No, don't call him. Wait, yes, do call him. I did it for him.

137

HE: You mean your husband put you up to pulling the robbery?

SHE: It's his fault. It's all his fault. The lazy buzzard.

HE: You mean he wouldn't do it himself?

SHE: Wouldn't do nothing for himself. I still have to cut his veal steak for him. After forty years of marriage, he still hasn't learned to cut the meat on his own plate. I cut it into tiny cubes, "bite size," he says. But still he don't say thank you. No, not once. Not one thank you in forty years of marriage.

HE (*Filling out report form*): Now, how much money did you get?

SHE: Almost two hundred.

HE: I have to know the exact amount.

SHE: A hundred eighty-five dollars. I got that from the Jay Hacock Mutual Life.

HE (*Fast and angry—a technique*): Were you also the hooded bandit who robbed the Murcury Loan Company of five hundred dollars on February twenty-eighth at four-thirty P.M.?

SHE: Don't shout at me.

HE: Sorry, ma'am. Just doing my job. This robbery you pulled was a lot like the one at Murcury.

SHE: What's murcury?

HE: I want you to identify the items I'm going to show

you. The matron removed them from you when we brought you in.

SHE: Where's my gun?

HE: I can't let you have it.

SHE (*Pitifully*): It isn't a real gun.

HE: It's evidence and belongs to the state.

SHE: What ever am I going to tell Stanley?

HE: Stanley?

SHE: My grandson, Stanley. He belongs to the track team, and that's the gun they use to start the races. He'll never forgive me.

HE: Please, ma'am, if you'll just pull yourself together and identify these things, I'll let you call Stanley to explain.

SHE: I'll try.

HE: Have you ever seen this black hood before?

SHE: Of course, I put it on in the washroom, before I went and robbed the insurance company. That's where I left my white hat.

HE: If you hadn't left that hat, we'd never have found you.

SHE: I don't care. Just wait till he gets home from work.

HE: Is this jacket . . . ?

SHE: Who'll cut up his meat in tiny cubes tonight, huh? Who do you think will do it?

HE: Is this jacket yours? Are these black slacks yours?

SHE: Yes. I bought them at our church rummage sale so you couldn't trace the labels.

HE: Where's the money?

SHE: What money?

HE: The hundred eighty-five you got away with.

SHE: Oh, that?

HE: Did you hide it in your home?

SHE: Now, that would be pretty dumb!

HE (*Intimately*): If we get the money back, the judge will go easy on you.

SHE: I don't want special treatment. Tell them to lock me up and swallow the key.

HE (*Fast and angry*): Where's the dough?

SHE: I won't tell.

HE: Please, lady, what'd you do with it?

SHE: I gave it away.

HE: You risked grand larceny to give the money away?

SHE: I put ten dollars in the hand of every bum on Third Avenue.

HE: The shit you did! Er, excuse me, ma'am.

SHE: Mister. When my husband comes to the station house, do you think, would you mind—I mean I'd like to borrow your handcuffs to wear for our interview. I know he'll carry on and try to hug me. But I want to be wearing those handcuffs so I won't have to hug him back.

(*A night club.*)

HE (*A comedian at a mike*): So these fuzz busted me and dragged me to the local jug. And the judge lays the rap on me, see. And he says to me I'm obscene, see. He says to me I'm obscene, that I talk dirty. That I talk sexy and arouse the aroused, that I don't know what I'm talking about, see, but if I didn't know what I'm talking about, how could I arouse all those dead dongs, see? And like the whole time I'm fishing my pocket for my pocket mirror and I gets it out and flash it at him, see. And I yells this is my sex detector Tester, see. And like he's nearsighted and I shove it right into his chops and I says, "If you're confused about sex," I says, I shove this here mirror right up to his whiskers, and the nose hairs of his nostrils tickle the top of the glass. And I says to him I says, "If you're confused about sex, yer honor, then hold this down to your crotch (unzipped, of course), and see if it'll mist up the glass. And if it don't, call in the firemen, cause you need a shot of novocaine in yer balls." And then he says to me . . .

SHE (*Drunk*): Go on home, yer mother's calling your mouth for soapysuds, dirty little boy.

HE: And then he says to me . . .

SHE: Out! With soap. Whyn't someone wash that loud mouth out with soap. He don't drink. He's too young.

HE: Will someone lay that broad in the mouth so that I can continue my dissertation?

SHE (*Jumping up with glass*): I'll do it myself. You mother!

HE (*Keeping mike between him and woman*): You get pimples that way, lady.

SHE (*Trying to hit him*): Stand still so I can put a stop to you.

HE: Husband? Husband of this drunk. Get up here. Your wife is making an ass of you.

SHE: Come here, you dirty rotten two-bit little East-side snot-snarf. I can teach you a lesson, if I could just reach you.

HE: Back to your table, cow pie.

SHE: Greaseball.

HE: You're so sloppy you have to home permanent your snatch.

SHE: Bastard, bastard.

HE: Beast, beast.

SHE: Bugger.

HE: Bug.

(*They become galaxies sending radio signals to each other.*)

SHE: Bleep Bleep. (*She moves in steady orbit.*)

HE (*Moving in a faster, more irregular orbit, sometimes slow, sometimes like a dervish, always in opposition to her rhythm*):Blink blink blink.

SHE: Bleep blink bleep blink bleep blink blink.

HE: Blink, blink, bleep bleep blink bleep bleep blink.

SHE: Bleep bleep blink blink bleep.

HE: Blink blink blink blink bleep blink blink bleep.

SHE: Bleep bleep bleep bleep blink bleep bleep blink.

HE (*Slowing*): Blink bleep blink.

SHE: Bleep blink bleep.

HE: Bleep bleep.

SHE: Blink blink.

HE: Bleep.

SHE: BLINK.

(*They come abreast and salute. They are members of a cub scout troup.*)

TOGETHER: ". . . and to the republic for which it stands, one nation indivisible, with liberty and justice for all." (*They put their hands like goggles over their eyes and sing*):

Up in the air, Junior Birdmen,
Up in the air upside down,
Up in the air, Junior Birdmen,
With your shoulders to the ground.

141

(*Chanting*):
It takes five wrappers,
Four box tops,
Three pop sticks,
Two bonbons,
One thin dime.

(*Singing*):
Up in the air, Junior Birdmen,
Up in the air upside down,
Up in the air, Junior Birdmen,
With your shoulders to the ground.

(SHE *looks far away, as if out to sea.* SHE *gestures to him to look too.* HE *comes close to her, and very slowly they sink to the floor and* SHE *pulls him on her lap and holds him as if he is a small boy.*)

SHE: Once upon a time when we lived on the beach we were hungry. You dug us a clam. You put the clam shell on a rock studded with white barnacles. We hid in a tide pool and waited for the sea gull to dive, feet first, at the clam. ZZZZZzzzzzzzzzzzzeeeeeeeeeeeeeeeeeeee, down came the gull and got the fat clam then dropped it from above and split the fat clam in two. We ran screaming to the rock and fought the sea gull for the fat juicy clam. And then we sat in the sand and ate and ate and ate and ate till the clam juice ran into our bellybuttons. That was the best clam we ever had.

HE: The best.

SHE: The absolute best.

(HE *pulls away from her, still crouching. They both pull blankets around them Indian style. They're huddling under a lean-to. It's cold.*)

SHE: Red feather.

HE: Mmmmmmmmmm.

SHE: Red feather.

HE: What?

SHE: Why are you silent?

HE: What is there to say?

SHE: Red feather?

HE: Yes.

SHE: Say it.

HE: Say what?

SHE: You want to go away from me.

HE: Maybe.

SHE: So go.

HE: In a while.

SHE: Then I'll go.

HE: All right.

SHE: Keep well.

HE: You too.

SHE: The sun is out.

HE: At last.

      (SHE *is arriving home after a long absence.*)

SHE: Dad?

HE: Who . . . is it . . . Sharon?

SHE: Yes.

HE: Sharon.

SHE: Yes.

HE: It's been a long time.

SHE: It doesn't seem like it now.

HE (*Looking at her face, pointing out some tiny lines*):
    You didn't have this one, or this one, or that
    one.

SHE: I know.

      (HE *pulls away.*)

SHE: Dad?

HE: Didn't get much fishing done. Water was too high
    this year, swept away all the eggs. Fish had
    a hell of a time trying to spawn too.

SHE: You sound the same.

HE: You don't.

SHE: How's the family?

HE: Same as ever.

SHE: You seem younger. I mean, *you* haven't changed.

HE: I guess not.

SHE: What is it?

HE: Eyes watering, that's all.

SHE: Can we take the boat out?

HE: Why, sure. Why, sure we can.

SHE: Let's go.

HE: Now?

SHE: Why not? It's been a long time.

HE: The tide's right.

SHE: Let's go.

HE: Like old times.

SHE: Like old times.

> (*A bedroom.* SHE *is packing and* HE *unpacks her things as* SHE *packs them.*)

HE: You're not leaving this house.

SHE: I can't help it.

HE: What do you mean you can't help it?

SHE: I can't. I can't help it.

HE: Of course you can help it. You can stay.

SHE: No.

HE: Don't say that. You can't say no to me. Not after all we've been through together. You can't walk out on me. We've survived everything, everything. You can't take that away. You can't leave.

SHE: I've got to.

HE: I forbid it. I forbid you to leave my bed.

SHE: That's why.

HE: That's why what? That's why what?

SHE: You're smothering me.

HE: You! I'm smothering you! Me! What about me? I'm the one who's been smothered around here, but I survived. I survived.

SHE: I can't help it. I'm sorry, but I can't stay.

HE: You're going to stay.

SHE: I can't. I can't help it.

HE: You're going to help it. You're going to face it. You're staying here.

SHE: I'm not.

HE: You are.

SHE: You disgust me.

HE: Big news.

SHE: You disgust me!

HE: And you know what you do to me?

SHE: I'm getting out.

HE: Not without me, you're not.

> (HE *picks her up and carries her to a rock near the ocean.* HE *wants her to give him a feeling of permanence. Repeat this scene three times.*)

HE: Have you known me long?

SHE: Yes.

HE: How long?

SHE: Long.

HE: How long?

SHE: Your eyes have green flecks at the center.

HE: How long?

SHE: Your nose has a small dimple here.

HE: Will you know me long?

SHE: Yes.

HE: How long?

SHE: Long.

HE: How long?

SHE: You have tufts of fur on your shoulder blades.

HE: You can never leave me.

SHE: I won't.

HE: How can I be sure?

SHE: You can be sure.

HE: How?

SHE: The bones of your feet remind me of dinosaurs.

HE: You do know me.

SHE: Yes.

HE: You do!

SHE: I do.

HE: You have known me.

SHE: Yes, it has been long.

HE (*Comforted*): You know me.

SHE: I know you.

> (*Jubilant,* HE *takes her hand and they leap to their feet and run with a leaping step to an open grassy field. This is based on a polka, a dance of joyous courtship.*)

HE: Inside.

SHE: Outside.

HE: All around.

SHE: Up and down.

HE: Turning.

SHE: Gliding.

HE: Inside.

SHE: Outside.

HE: Right along.

SHE: Galloping.

HE: Jump.

SHE: Catch me.

HE: Sweet.

SHE: Hard.

HE: Hold on.

SHE: Tight.

HE: Upsadaisy.

SHE: Inside.

HE: Outside.

SHE: Shall we go in?

HE: Right away.

SHE: Inside?

HE: IN!

> (*All the actors join together for the final scene. This should be carefully staged and played warmly to the audience. It is to be sung and gracefully danced.*)

HE: Haven't I met you somewhere before?
On the steps of Elsinore?

At the film of Eleanor?
Just inside the Barbary Shore?

SHE: No, no no, I don't think so,
Although I'd like to slip with you behind the
door.

HE: What more, what more, what more
Could any man ask of a new maid?

SHE: Then shall we slip,
Then shall we dip,
Into a love time,
Travel to a hot clime?

HE: What more, what more, what more
Could any man ask of a new maid?

TOGETHER:
Then we'll dip,
We'll slip,
We'll glide,
We'll hide.
We'll slide
Into love time,
Into love time,
Into love time.

Then we'll dip,
We'll slip,
We'll glide,
We'll hide.
We'll slide

Into love time,
Into love time,
Into love time.

Love time,
Love time,
Love time,
Love time,

INTO LOVE TIME!

CURTAIN

KEEP TIGHTLY CLOSED IN A COOL DRY PLACE

■

For Joseph Chaikin

PRODUCTION NOTES

∎

There are as many ways to approach this play as there are combinations of four people who might involve themselves in it. Each time I've seen the play performed I've learned more about it. Rehearsals of the play have been fascinating and absorbing in the same way but to a different degree than the performance. The actors must face themselves and must reveal themselves to one another to do the play at all. The director shares in this: he guides and explores, contributes his own passions, obsessions, and hang-ups. If all can contribute with courage, they'll be rewarded by considerable enrichment of their professional technique and personal awareness.

The play can be directed literally or as a fantasy or dream. The director should decide his approach, but he should take the actors into his confidence and readjust his ideas according to the personalities and technical level of his men.

The director should decide if a murder *has* been committed, or if it is the desire *to* commit the murder, or if it is a dramatization of relief—a relief at having faced the ultimate crime that this one man could conceive of according to his limitations, designing and submitting, and then forgiving himself for this crime. Did he do it or not? The challenge of the play, aside from the doing of it, is to decide between the four involved, the director and the players, what matters to you. Then use the material to show and resolve this to your audience.

The play can be wildly funny—don't be frightened of this.

The three men can also be seen as aspects of one personality. In performing from this standpoint it is advisable for the director to design exercises of dependence, isolation, and impact. The actors must come to understand that they are connected with one another by muscle, blood vessels, and nervous structure—impulses felt by one member may be enacted by another. This should bring about a closeness in the playing that will enhance the play, be enjoyable to the actors and thus especially rewarding to the audience.

The men should be dressed in identical work clothes, either blue or green. Three army cots can be used for the beds, but an enlarged playing area is obtained with a strong double bunk and one single.

KEEP TIGHTLY CLOSED IN A COOL DRY PLACE

■

JASPERS, *an intense, intelligent, and arrogant lawyer in his thirties.*

MICHAELS, *a burly, coarse, heavy-shouldered man looking to get ahead.*

GREGORY, *a handsome, well-built young man with a bewildered mouth.*

(*A jail cell for three. Two bunks and one single bed are the only furniture. The men face the audience in a row in front of the beds. They combine to become a machine.*)

MICHAELS: Press here . . .

GREGORY: Tear back . . .

JASPERS: To replace . . .

TOGETHER (*Locking arms*): Insert lip. But we may be opened. But we may be opened. But we may be opened for . . .

JASPERS: For inspection.

> (*Their bodies become ultra tense. They move in a military manner and climb into the bunks and put the pillows under their heads. They sleep.*)

JASPERS (*Waking and sitting bolt-upright*): Mike! Mike!

MICHAELS (*Slow and depressed*): What?

JASPERS: Are you all right?

MICHAELS: No. I'm in jail.

JASPERS: Do you feel good?

MICHAELS: No. I'm in jail.

JASPERS: What's wrong with you?

MICHAELS: I told you. I'm in jail.

JASPERS: Try to feel good.

MICHAELS: I can't. I'm in jail.

JASPERS: Think good. Stay healthy. We've got to get out. We can't give up. We'll become jelly.

MICHAELS: I don't feel good.

JASPERS: You said that.

MICHAELS: Do you feel good?

JASPERS: Wound tight. We gotta get out of here.

MICHAELS: How?

JASPERS: We're innocent.

MICHAELS: We tried that line already.

JASPERS: We're innocent. (*Whispering*) Shut it, you stupe, they've probably got the cell bugged.

MICHAELS: I don't feel good.

JASPERS: Is Gregory asleep?

MICHAELS: He's always asleep.

JASPERS: How can he sleep so much?

MICHAELS: He said he never used to sleep before.

JASPERS: We'll get him to confess.

MICHAELS: He already did.

JASPERS: We'll make him confess he lied.

MICHAELS: But he didn't . . .

JASPERS: What was I telling you about how he lied! Shut up!

MICHAELS: I'm a sick man. You shouldn't shout at a guy who don't feel good.

JASPERS: Get up.

MICHAELS: I can't.

JASPERS: Get up.

MICHAELS: I can't.

JASPERS: Get up.

MICHAELS: My legs ache.

JASPERS: Get up.

MICHAELS: My feet don't feel good.

JASPERS: Stand up.

MICHAELS: I can't.

JASPERS: Shit! Get out of that bed!

MICHAELS: You get up first.

JASPERS: Do you want your share or not?

MICHAELS: I got my share and I don't like it.

JASPERS: You still working for me or not?

MICHAELS: I don't know you.

JASPERS: Cut that out.

MICHAELS: You spent all your time in court proving we didn't know each other.

JASPERS: Do you want to get out of here?

MICHAELS: How can we get out? We were even denied an appeal.

JASPERS: We can get a new trial if we uncover new evidence.

MICHAELS: There ain't nothing new.

JASPERS: There's going to be.

MICHAELS: You're stir crazy already.

JASPERS: That's the difference between us. I never give up. That's why you don't feel good and I'm ready to start again. I feel good. I feel good enough to get out of here. I got my boys to bring up.

MICHAELS: How can you? You didn't even get the insurance money.

JASPERS: My sons are not going to live out their childhood as wards of the state. They'll grow into something like Gregory here.

MICHAELS: What can you do? You didn't get a cent. You're broke, you son of a bitch.

JASPERS: I didn't go through all this hell for nothing.

MICHAELS: That D.A. made you look like the amateur you are.

JASPERS: If you're so good at spotting amateurs, why did you go along with it?

MICHAELS: You dazzled me. You duped me with your smart talk.

JASPERS: Gregory will confess.

MICHAELS: To what?

JASPERS: That he implicated us to save his own skin. That he doesn't know us. The state produced no witness that ever saw any of us together. I'll make Gregory confess and I'll be acquitted.

MICHAELS: You! What about me?

JASPERS: You don't feel good, remember? You might as well stay in here and get well at the state's expense.

MICHAELS: You ain't getting out without me.

JASPERS: You aren't getting out *with* me, if you don't get off your butt and help me.

MICHAELS (*Painfully rising from bunk*): What we gonna do?

JASPERS: We'll make him sign a confession.

MICHAELS: He'll never do that. He already turned State's Evidence.

JASPERS: Well, he can re-turn. Why would anyone believe a convicted ex-con murderer?

MICHAELS: Because he told the truth.

JASPERS: What did I tell you? Your mouth! That's it. That's it with you. You're fired! Out!

MICHAELS: Don't get your balls in an uproar. I'll help you. I'll help, but I don't think he'll give in.

JASPERS: We'll make him.

MICHAELS: How?

JASPERS: Torture.

MICHAELS: The guards . . .

JASPERS: Don't worry about them.

MICHAELS: How can you . . . ?

JASPERS: Shut up. I'll teach you. Get him on his feet.

MICHAELS (*Pulls* GREGORY *out of bed*): Yes, sir!

JASPERS (*Changes into General Custer, buckles on sword, tips hat forward, climbs on horse, gallops in circle, comes back to* MICHAELS): Tie that redskin up.

MICHAELS (*Becomes a bluecoat*): Yes, sir! (*He stands* GREGORY *up against a post.*)

GREGORY (*As Indian Chief, his hands and feet tied*): Prairie dogs! (*He spits at the two men.*) Women. Girls. (*Bellows like a buffalo.*) Pretty bonnets. Yellow ribbons!

JASPERS (*Drawling*): Cut out that redskin's tongue.

MICHAELS: Yes, sir!

GREGORY (*Laughing derisively*): Ten thousand knives cannot stop White Fang.

JASPERS: Blow the death call. That'll frighten him.

MICHAELS: Yes, sir! (*Sounds like a bugle.*)

GREGORY: I'll never sign the treaty. This is our land. Cut me. Shred me into pemmican, but a hundred historians and *Life* magazine will tell the world of your cowardly crimes.

JASPERS: Cut off that redskin's ear.

GREGORY: Lice, you virus bearers, you smallpox carriers, you jerking instruments of VD.

JASPERS (*Drawling*): Cut off that redskin's other ear.

MICHAELS: Yes, sir!

GREGORY (*Singing an Indian death chant*):
> I have scalped more scalps than any scalper
> of my tribe. I,
> White Fang, Chief of the Dakotas,
> Have broken and ridden the Spanish horses
> Over the whitemen's wives and raped them
> with my redskin.

JASPERS: Cut off that bastard's balls.

GREGORY (*Singing*):
> Cold turds, creeping cruds, shocking pinks,
> Blue baboons, red lagoons, Hoffa's raccoons.
> Subway feelers, public peelers . . .
> White Fang, Chief of the Dakotas spits on you.

MICHAELS: Get his tongue for Custer! Get his balls for Custer!

JASPERS (*Drawling*): Save his song for Ruth Benedict and the *National Geographic*. (GREGORY *faints from pain, pulls his blanket over him. He's half covered on the floor.*)

JASPERS (*Dismounting from his horse and putting on his shirt*): Get him on his feet, Mike.

MICHAELS: You do it.

JASPERS: Do you want to get out of here or don't you?

MICHAELS: Sure I do.

JASPERS: Then do what I say.

MICHAELS: Puke on the day I was thick enough to listen to you to start with.

JASPERS: If you hadn't been so stupid as to hire an amateur . . .

MICHAELS: He's an ex-Marine. A sharp shooter.

JASPERS: Then why did it take so long to kill my wife?

MICHAELS: He told me he could do the job.

JASPERS: Hearsay . . . you went on hearsay . . . hearsay from a mouth, from the defendant's own mouth. You should have had proof.

MICHAELS: Well, how was I supposed to get proof? Make him kill some broad in front of my eyes to test his quality control?

JASPERS: Before you call me on *my* judgment, I want you to review yours. I could have hired a hood from the East to do it right.

MICHAELS: But look what it'd have cost you. We saved nearly twenty grand by getting Greg.

JASPERS: That was your idea, and look where we are.

MICHAELS: I don't feel so good.

JASPERS: You won't get better by rotting here. Listen to me. I want you to make him cry.

MICHAELS: Him? Don't make me laugh. He never cried in his life.

JASPERS: He's going to. He's going to. You're going to make him.

MICHAELS: How?

JASPERS: I'll teach you. And after he's had all the hate you can give him, I'll take over and give him love.

MICHAELS: Wait a minute . . . wait a minute . . .

JASPERS: Brotherly love . . . brotherly.

MICHAELS: I don't like the sound in your voice.

JASPERS: Relax and follow my plan.

MICHAELS: Do you really think you can get him to sign a paper saying he lied about us?

JASPERS: I know I can.

MICHAELS: All right. I'll give him a try.

JASPERS: First, make him feel small.

MICHAELS (*Looking down at* GREGORY): He's got one again.

JASPERS: Wake him up.

MICHAELS: He's smiling.

JASPERS: He's having a dream without us. Wake him up!

MICHAELS: This guy's got a hard-on for the whole world. How can I make him feel small when he can get that big? (*He shakes* GREGORY.)

GREGORY: Don't stop. Don't stop.

JASPERS: Tell me who it is?

GREGORY: Who, what?

JASPERS: Your dream. You're having a dream, you selfish bastard.

MICHAELS: Share with us Gregory. Tell us.

GREGORY: Tell what?

JASPERS: You know what I'm talking about, you potent son-of-a-bitch.

GREGORY: I'm going back to sleep.

MICHAELS: You're not. You're gonna tell us your dream.

JASPERS: Start over. You can do it.

GREGORY: That's no good.

JASPERS: You can—any hour, any day. I never saw such a stud.

GREGORY: I can't tell it.

JASPERS: You got to.

GREGORY: I don't know how. There's no words.

JASPERS: There's pictures. Tell me the pictures. Tell us what you see yourself doing?

GREGORY: I'm in the subway.

JASPERS and MICHAELS: Yeah.

GREGORY: I got her coming off the subway. Deserted part of the platform.

MICHAELS: Then where?

GREGORY: Phone booth, under the farthest stairs.

167

JASPERS: What she look like?

GREGORY: Light blonde. Little curls, tiny wrinkles. Cute nose. Not enough mouth, but that's okay. I'm not going for the mouth.

JASPERS: Your knife. Where's your knife?

GREGORY: I tear down her blouse, then I flip my knife and cut one bra strap and then I cut the other bra strap.

JASPERS: Then her slip. Take off her slip.

GREGORY: She ain't wearing no slip.

MICHAELS: Grab or bite?

GREGORY: I squeeze them hard. She gasps, but I shove my tongue down her throat so she can't make no noise. Then I tear down her skirt and lean hard on her front, then I take my knife and cut one garter and then I cut the other garter. Then I take my knife and slash her girdle down the middle of her belly. I hold the knife to the belly button and tell her, "undo my fly, or I'll shove this knife right up your gut." She puts her shaking hands on my zipper and ahhhhhhhhhhh . . . good good good good good nice yes yes . . . (*He comes and lies back, moaning under his blanket.*)

MICHAELS: There goes the ball game!

JASPERS: Stupid grammar-school back-alley punk! No wonder you got caught. You don't know how to finish anything!

(JASPERS *and* MICHAELS *climb angrily back into their bunks.*)

GREGORY (*Alone, he rises from the floor during his speech*): This girl on our street, she used to drink water from the swamp on her way home from school . . . and she swallowed tons of this here water . . . and one day she was swallowing the water and it was loaded with snake eggs and she didn't know it . . . and she swallowed this snake egg . . . BUT SHE DIDN'T KNOW IT . . . and nobody else knew it. 'Cause everyone just thought it was plain water, but this here snake egg was too small to see, see? And then this girl she got skinnier and skinnier, until she was just bones except for her little belly which was round and tight as a basketball. The last day of her life she was laying on her bed in her bedroom, see, and her grandmother was trying to make her eat, see, and her dad was trying to make her eat some of this here soup. And she just stared up at them. She was dead, get it. But they didn't get it yet. And they's all banded about her bed waving these here spoons and dishes . . . and they keep pleading her to eat this good grub and that. Finally her old man grabs her jaws and forces them open. Guess who sticks a tongue out at him? Yeah. Guess who? Yeah! It was the snake. It was the snake grown up! (*He looks at audience a moment and then becomes withdrawn.*) Don't be nice to me. I

169

can't stand that. Don't be nice to me or I'll bite! (*Hissing and moving snakelike, he gets to center stage. The men group to become a machine.*)

TOGETHER: The world's most dependable.

JASPERS: Featuring full-time control.

TOGETHER: Rugged! Versatile! Smooth!

GREGORY: Guaranteed. Precision locked.

MICHAELS: Easy to operate.

JASPERS: Visible refill.

TOGETHER: Heavy duty.

GREGORY: De luxe. Easy to load.

TOGETHER: Push in and pull down and push in.

JASPERS: Assured smooth uninterrupted performance.

MICHAELS: Versatility of operation.

GREGORY: Easy to get at mechanism.

TOGETHER: SAFE!

MICHAELS: Prevents banged-up fingers.

JASPERS: Insured against jamming . . .

GREGORY: . . . AND clogging. Safe!

TOGETHER: Self closing!

(*The three spring back to bed.*)

JASPERS (*Leaps out of bed and confronts* GREGORY):

Tell me! You tell me how you murdered my wife. You say you did it. You told the police, the judge, the jury, and my children how you murdered my wife. Now it's time you told me.

GREGORY: You were there.

JASPERS: Where was I? I was at work. I was in my office working on a brief when you were in my house killing my wife. I want you to stand right there. See that spot on the floor? I want you to stand right there.

MICHAELS: Stand there.

GREGORY: I'm sleepy.

JASPERS: Put him on that spot, Michaels.

MICHAELS (*Grabbing* GREGORY): On this spot.

GREGORY (*Pointing at* MICHAELS): He paid me to do it. A lousy two thousand bills.

JASPERS: What was that? I didn't hear you. Speak up. You're in a court of law. You speak up and show respect for the people of your society who are trying you here today. What was that? What was that you mumbled there?

MICHAELS: Open your gap and tell your story.

GREGORY: You son-of-a-bitch, you're the one what hired me to do it.

MICHAELS: I never saw you before in my life. And you tell it here today. You never saw me before in your life.

171

JASPERS: Are the paper and pen ready?

GREGORY: What for?

JASPERS: Your confession.

MICHAELS: Ready.

GREGORY: I already confessed. I confessed and signed it.

JASPERS: You confessed and signed a lie.

GREGORY: I didn't lie.

JASPERS: But we're going to give you a chance to redeem yourself. You can sign a retraction.

GREGORY: I don't know what you're talking about.

JASPERS: You just say that your story is a lie. That you acted alone.

GREGORY: You're stew-brained. I ain't taking the rap for you.

JASPERS: You're going to write a sweet letter. You're going to write a letter to the Governor telling him you lied. You're going to tell him I did not hire Michaels to hire you to kill my wife. That neither Michaels nor I know you. You alone executed the murder. You took the mother of my children away from them. You write about your murder. It belongs to you alone. Your murder. The murder that you committed four times to finish my valiant wife, the murder that trailed blood from my kitchen to the front-door mat back through the hall, up the stairs to the upstairs and into the bathroom, and pooled on the floor and spattered on the white tub and finally clogged the bathtub drain. That is the murder that you are going to confess to. That is the murder that you are going to write a sweet letter to the Governor about. That is the murder you hacked yourself, all by yourself with my kitchen knife, you awkward, clumsy stupid snot-minded moron. That is the unprofessional murder that you committed and dragged me through all the courts of this state. So that you wouldn't be alone. A stupid crumb, a minuscule brain, a pulsating slug, a meat-handed pig, a stinking misfit like you could bring me down. All right. So I'm in the same cell. So you brought me into your world! But now you are damn well going to get me out again.

GREGORY: You can't make me sign anything.

JASPERS: You'll sign it. You will. Yes, you will please sign it. (*He feels suddenly ill.*) My throat's so dry. Please sign. You will. Say . . . (*He sinks to floor and pulls* GREGORY's *blanket around him.*) So bloody cold . . . (*He becomes a fifteen-year-old English lad, dying in the first swamps of Jamestown, Virginia. He coughs, and shivers, and moans.*) Please, water . . . a taste . . . only one . . . then I'll ask for nothing more . . . a drop . . .

MICHAELS (*Wrapping himself in blanket*): Half the force died in the night.

JASPERS: Where's our captain . . . ? I want Captain Smith.

MICHAELS: That lying black heart! I hope he's croaked.

JASPERS: Not him. Not Smith. He's not the dying kind.

MICHAELS: We are all the dying kind.

JASPERS: Captain Smith'll get us to higher ground.

MICHAELS: Not while that old fool Speedgood can still snort.

JASPERS: He's not still alive? Not that old pisspot!

MICHAELS: Last I saw was him crashing across the flaming dawn, his matted white hair spattered with blood and vomit. He had his sword in two hands and was poking the dying, roaring at them to rise and build a glorious new city for the Queen. They'll have a fine time roasting his withered balls in hell.

JASPERS: We've failed Raleigh. He trusted us.

MICHAELS: He shouldn't-a picked such marsh minds to head the expedition then. He'll be throwing himself into the Thames. We've lost every pound sterling old Queen Bess advanced him.

JASPERS: One thing I'm grateful for . . .

MICHAELS: Curse the day I signed on this voyage!

JASPERS: I'm not hungry any more.

GREGORY (*Wrapped in blanket. He is John Smith*):
Lad? Where are you, lad?

174

JASPERS: Here, sir.

GREGORY (*Holding out cup*): Water. Be careful, 'tis hot, lad. I boiled it from the muddy swamp.

MICHAELS: You liar, Smith. You bragging boasting son-of-a-pigging liar!

GREGORY: He's possessed!

MICHAELS: I'm possessed enough of my senses to tell you what I think of you and your get-rich-quick schemes. You and that filthy tobacco seller Raleigh!

GREGORY: Hush, man. I'll run you through if you speak against Sir Walter.

MICHAELS: Do it. Get me over with. I won't live till dawn anyway.

GREGORY: Here, lad. Drink.

JASPERS: My teeth's chattering too much to get it to my mouth.

GREGORY (*Holding him*): You do as you're told.

JASPERS (*Drinks and coughs*): Any sign of a ship, sir?

GREGORY: I've built a big signal fire on the beach. Raleigh won't forsake us.

MICHAELS: He won't come. He won't throw good money after bad.

JASPERS: I see a ship, sir.

GREGORY: Where?

JASPERS: In the bay, sir. She's trimming sail, to put in. Someone's waving to us, from the deck.

GREGORY: Who?

JASPERS: Elizabeth. The Queen, sir. She's waving to us. We're saved.

GREGORY: You're shaking all over.

JASPERS: If I could only stand. I've got to meet her. Hold me up, sir.

GREGORY (*Holding him*): I'll hold you fast. I'll keep you from God and the Devil. I'll save you for the Queen.

JASPERS: Take me there.

GREGORY: Hang onto me, damn your eyes. Hang onto me. Hang onto me. You didn't get your chance yet. Hang on. Hang on.

MICHAELS (*Rises and covers them with blanket and folds himself in with them. The three men move in circular motion under the blankets. They call.*)

TOGETHER: Hold me. Hold me. Hold me. Keep us. Close us. Dust to dust. Ashes to ashes, dust to dust. (*The slow beat changes to a faster one. They punch the blanket from the inside and sing slowly and then the beat picks up.*)

Dust to dust, dust to dust. Ashes to ashes, dust to dust, ashes to ashes, dust to dust. (*They rise. Still under the blanket they lock arms and move in a simple dance step.*)

Asses to asses, dust to dust. Two twin beds but only one of them mussed.

"Now you can easily see she's not my mother, 'cause my mother's forty-nine. And you can easily see she's not my sister, 'cause I'd never give my sister such a hell of a good time!"

(*Singing*):
Many's a night I spent with Minnie the Mermaid down at the bottom of the sea.
Down amongst the coral, there I lost my morals,
Gee, but she was good to me.
Asses to asses, dust to dust,
Two twin beds but only one of them mussed.
(*They throw off blankets.*)

Now you can easily see she's not my girlfriend
Cause my girlfriend's too refined.
She's just a hell of a sweet kid who never cared what she did,
She's a personal friend of mine.
Roll over, Minnie.
It's softer on the other side.

(*The men break and, military fashion, replace the blankets smartly on their beds.* GREGORY *seems to be hiding something. He tries to swallow it, but* JASPERS *catches him and takes it away from him.*)

JASPERS (*Showing* MICHAELS *a paper. The men talk and pose like drag queens*): Look at this. What is

177

this? (*To* GREGORY) Why were you trying to swallow this paper?

GREGORY: None of your frigging business.

JASPERS (*With* MICHAELS, *plays keep-away with the note*): I do believe our little girl was trying to swallow a love note.

MICHAELS: Her pretty skin's been getting the long drink looks in the mess hall every day.

JASPERS: Don't tease her now. That's mean. Don't make her pretty cheeks get all red with burning embarrassment. That's no fun is it, Ava baby?

GREGORY: Don't call me Ava! I hate that hole! She can't even act.

JASPERS: But she bats a million in the sex department. Just like you, Kim baby. That's better! You like that better? Yes, she likes that better. Look at her mouth. She's on the verge of smiling. Yes, she is. Let it go. You won't crack that pretty face. Here, go on, let's have it all. Let's have that nice smile now. All the way, that's a good Kim baby.

MICHAELS: Fer Christ's sake! (*Snatching note and reading.*) "Roses are red, violets are blue, Yez's sweeter 'n' sugar, that's why I wanna get next to you. Signed the Swinging Woolf."

GREGORY (*Diving for note*): That's why I wanted to get rid of it. It's terrible. It's not even original.

JASPERS: Oh, I don't know. A Swinging Woolf can't be *all* bad. Here, Michaels, let me see it?

GREGORY: It's mine.

JASPERS: I thought you put it down.

GREGORY: Just the same, it was sent to me. I can do as I please with it.

JASPERS: It's community property. It was sent to this cell. How do you know it was meant for you? Maybe the Swinging Woolf meant to send it to Michaels here?

MICHAELS: I'll bust you wide open!

JASPERS: Or maybe he has a crush on me. Since when did you get so conceited, Gregory? What mirrors you been looking in, right, Mike?

MICHAELS: Yeah. Who'd want that carcass . . .

GREGORY: I'm only twenty-four.

MICHAELS: Says you! What does your birth certificate say? Look at his nose, Jaspers. Can you stand soberly and say it's sweet?

JASPERS: Turn your head, Kimmie. I want to see the profile.

MICHAELS: A hunky nose if I ever saw one.

GREGORY: I'm no hunky. My father was German and my mother was . . .

MICHAELS: A whore.

GREGORY: Don't you say anything against . . .

MICHAELS: She did it for money and you do it for candy and cigarettes.

GREGORY (*Abruptly changes from drag queen to movie gangster*): What's with you? Get off my back. I thought you was my friend.

MICHAELS (*Abruptly changes to movie gangster also*): Shows how crazy you really are. I was never your friend.

GREGORY: You bought me drinks. You paid my rent all those months while we planned the murder . . .

MICHAELS: You're the one did it. I didn't do nothing, so a few drinks. I buy lots of slobs drinks when I want a few laughs.

GREGORY: Some laugh. You're in for life for a few laughs. You aren't laughing now.

MICHAELS: Neither are you, little darling of the state.

GREGORY: I wasn't gonna take the rap alone.

MICHAELS: You was paid to.

GREGORY: They woulda given me the chair if I hadn't told the truth.

MICHAELS: Nobody gets the chair any more. Smart lawyers like Jaspers here can get you off. If I got to spend the rest of my life with you, I'm gonna make sure you don't enjoy it.

GREGORY: I don't get it. Why don't you finks let me sleep? All I want to do is sleep. I never had it so good.

MICHAELS: Go on. Go on, baby blue. Climb in your bunk and get some shuteye. If you dare to close them sweetsie peepers, that is.

GREGORY: What could you do? You can't do nothing to me. Nothing, do you hear me?

MICHAELS: My, my, she does get excited. No wonder she's such a crumby amateur.

GREGORY: You can't do nothing. What could you do?

MICHAELS: That's for me to know and you to find out.

GREGORY: I'm not afraid of you.

MICHAELS: When you least expect it. When you least expect it, that's when you'll hear from me.

GREGORY: Get off my back. I'm not afraid of you. You middleman. You're just jealous. Me. I done it. I'm the one that did it. I didn't know she was so strong. Who ever knew a little woman could be so strong. She got to the front door-mat after I'd strangled her with the cord, and she pulled me the whole way. I barely was able to keep her from crawling to the yard. I crushed her right hand in the door hinge and tried to bang her temples with the metal knob. But she kicked my crotch and staggered up the stairs. Then I had her. I tackled her outside the bathroom door and stabbed her fifty-seven times with the steak knife. But she was still breathing. That son-of-a-bitch Michaels wouldn't let me use a gun. I used a gun in Korea all right and never had no trouble in making anybody stay dead. There was so much frigging blood it was gushing down the stairs. And she was still breathing and her arms was lashing at me. I dumped her in the bathtub and opened her mouth under the faucet and turned the water on full blast. Then I ran like hell.

MICHAELS: You should return the money. What a botch.

GREGORY: She's dead, ain't she? Isn't that what he wanted?

MICHAELS: He wanted the half-million insurance money, you lousy crumb.

GREGORY: Well, she's dead. He wanted her dead. She's dead.

MICHAELS: What good is it?

GREGORY: I did it. You wanted her dead? So I did it. She's dead.

MICHAELS: What good is it? What good is it?

GREGORY: I did what you wanted me to do. I did it. What more could I do?

MICHAELS: Don't you have no conscience? What good is it? What good is it that she's dead and we don't have the money? What a waste. Look at what a waste you made. A waste is a waste is a waste. That's what you are! You, Gregory, are a total loss. A total loss. A nothing. Nothing but a nothing.

GREGORY: Get off my back. You didn't do anything. You really didn't do anything. Get off my back. You're just jealous.

MICHAELS: Listen at that high-pitched hysterical voice. Listen at that stupid screaming total loss.

GREGORY: My voice is not high.

MICHAELS: My voice is not high.

GREGORY: It's not.

MICHAELS: It's not.

GREGORY: Cut it out, you frigging tight-ass.

MICHAELS: Cut it out, you frigging tight-ass.

GREGORY: Oh, I get it. You're just trying to bug me.

MICHAELS: You're just trying to bug me.

GREGORY: I don't fall for that old game.

MICHAELS: I don't fall for that old game.

GREGORY: You can't make me crack.

MICHAELS: You can't make me crack.

GREGORY: Copy me all you want. Don't you wish you could.

MICHAELS: Don't you wish you could.

GREGORY: Won't get you anywhere.

MICHAELS: Won't get you anywhere.

GREGORY: No fart-nosed, messenger boy can . . .

MICHAELS: No fart-nosed, messenger boy can . . .

GREGORY: Jaspers, make him stop.

MICHAELS: Jaspers, make him stop.

GREGORY: You're just trying to make me hit you . . .

MICHAELS: Just trying to make me hit you . . .

GREGORY: So you can yell for the screw!

MICHAELS: So you can yell for the screw!

GREGORY (*Shouting in spite of himself*): I won't yell.

MICHAELS (*Whispering*): I won't yell.

GREGORY: (*Breaking into sobs, he throws himself on bunk*): You first-class prick.

MICHAELS: You second-class cunt.

> (GREGORY *breaks down all the way and hangs his head on side of bunk.*)

JASPERS (*Motions* MICHAELS *to stand back and goes to* GREGORY. *Puts hand on shoulder. He talks like Bogart or Cagney*): Hey. Hey. There, there, big boy. What is it? That's no way to do. Hey. Someone get your goat? Here. Let me see. Look at me. That's a boy. Big hunk like you crying. Who'd believe it? (*Gives him a playful cuff.*) That's better, calm down. Don't pay any attention to Mike. He's an insensitive slob. But not you. You're sensitive. You're a sensitive kid.

GREGORY: I'll kill him. I'll kill him. He can't make me feel like this and live. Nobody can.

JASPERS: He ain't worth killing. He don't understand sensitivity. Wouldn't make any impression on him to kill him.

GREGORY: Clod. He don't understand high-strung people.

JASPERS: No, he doesn't. That's right. But I do. You know I do, don't you? If I get out of here, then I can get you out.

GREGORY: No, you can't. I signed a confession.

JASPERS: I'll prove that the police beat the confession out of you. We'll void the confession. Here, sign this for me.

GREGORY: What is it?

JASPERS: Just a paper to help me get out of here.

GREGORY: Oh no. Oh no you don't. I may be upset, but I'm not crazy. I'm not signing anything that'll be good for that shit, Michaels.

JASPERS: He doesn't count. Don't even think about him.

GREGORY: I won't sign.

JASPERS: You're too upset to think about it now, Gregory. Just rest awhile. We'll talk about it another time.

GREGORY: I won't sign.

JASPERS: Greg. There's something I've been wondering about.

GREGORY: What . . .

JASPERS: What did it feel like?

GREGORY: To kill . . . to kill your wife . . . ?

JASPERS: Not exactly. I can imagine that. I've lived it so often. No . . . what did it feel like . . . what did it feel like to her do you suppose . . .

GREGORY: How should I know? I never been killed before . . .

(MICHAELS *changes into a small boy.* JASPERS *becomes his dead wife working in the kitchen rolling out pie dough.*)

MICHAELS (*An eight-year-old*): Mommie. Mommie.

JASPERS: What is it, Richard?

MICHAELS: There's a man at the door.

JASPERS: Don't answer it.

MICHAELS: I'm sorry. I'm sorry, Mommie, but I already did.

JASPERS: Dickie, how many times has your daddy told you not to answer the door?

MICHAELS: I know, Mommie. I'm sorry I forgot. I heard the bell ring and I'd opened the door before I knew it, and there was a great great great big man standing at the door, smiling.

JASPERS: Smiling?

MICHAELS: Like this. He was smiling like this. And he punched me one.

JASPERS: He punched you.

MICHAELS: I fooled you, I fooled Mommie. Not a hard punch stupid Mother. I fooled you. What a dumb mother!

JASPERS: Richard, don't speak to Mother like that.

MICHAELS: Dumb Mother, dumb Mother, dumb Mother.

JASPERS: Richie, don't say things like that. I'm right in the middle of preparing a quiche Lorraine for your father.

MICHAELS: I fooled you. I fooled you. What a dumb woman you are.

JASPERS: Richard!

MICHAELS: I'm going back to the man at the door. He's smarter than you are.

JASPERS: I don't believe there's anyone at the door.

MICHAELS: No. You're right. There's no one at the door.

JASPERS: I thought not.

MICHAELS: No, there's no one at the door.

JASPERS: You and your imagination. I wish your father wouldn't encourage that imagination of yours.

MICHAELS: No, there's no one at the door. He's standing right behind you.

187

GREGORY (*Carrying a small cord*): Mrs. Jaspers?

JASPERS: Oh! You startled me. I didn't know you were there.

GREGORY: Didn't your boy tell you?

JASPERS: No. Yes. Well, he tells me so many things.

GREGORY: You're Wynona Jaspers?

JASPERS: Yes. Yes, I am. You see my father was named Winthrop and I was supposed to be Winthrop Jr. so they . . .

GREGORY: Your husband is Frank Jaspers, attorney?

JASPERS: Yes. Who are you?

GREGORY (*Snapping the cord against his leg*): Friend of your husband's. I'd like to talk with you about him.

JASPERS: What about?

GREGORY: I have information you might be interested in.

JASPERS: What sort of information?

GREGORY: Like . . . what he does those nights he works late at the office night after night after night after night after . . .

JASPERS: Richard, go outside and play with your brother.

MICHAELS (*Pointing at* GREGORY): I want to play with him.

JASPERS: Richard, go get Mark. He's next door at Goodman's.

MICHAELS: And can I come right back?

JASPERS: Yes.

GREGORY: No.

> (GREGORY *stalks* JASPERS *with a cord. They circle in a slow tense dance.* GREGORY *gets the cord around* JASPERS' *neck and forces him back onto his bunk. He pulls the cord as tight as he can.* JASPERS *fights, then relaxes. An exhausted* GREGORY *makes for his own bed.*)

JASPERS (*Calling from his bed in a hoarse whisper*): Michaels?

MICHAELS: Yeah?

JASPERS: How are you feeling?

MICHAELS: Why?

JASPERS: I don't like you not to feel good.

MICHAELS: Thanks.

JASPERS: Michaels?

MICHAELS: Yeah?

JASPERS: Are you feeling better?

MICHAELS: A bit.

JASPERS: Michaels?

MICHAELS: Yeah?

JASPERS: Come and get in bed with me.

MICHAELS: The guard.

JASPERS: That screw's on his coffee break.

MICHAELS: I'm not my old self.

JASPERS: Let's have each other.

MICHAELS: O.K.

JASPERS: I'm too tense. My mind's jammed. Clear it for me.

MICHAELS: (*Climbing from his into* JASPERS' *bed*): Gotta be quiet or they'll separate us for sure. (*Stands at head of bed and rubs* JASPERS' *head. Alone.*) There, there. There, there. Don't be scared. (*He stops. Pause, smiles at audience.*) Don't be upset. (*He tiptoes toward audience.*) I'm gonna sing you a story . . . Once upon a time there lived an old witch, and she lived right in the middle of my forehead . . . And she was bad, oh cats, she was bad, and she sat in the middle of my forehead. Now the blood ran red, and it ran down her nose, and she stirred it in her cauldron, and she stirred it with her toes, right in the middle of my forehead. (*Kneels downstage—breathes and moves in rhythm with* JASPERS, *who remains in bed.*)

JASPERS (*Alone on his bunk, he's going toward sexual climax*): Yes. Yes. I'm ready. I'm ready to receive. Yes. Yes. I can go one step further. Yes. I'll do it. I can I will, I'll do it. I'll transmit it. Yes . . . yes . . . ready, Roger, Eddie . . . Directive: Amalgamated Vesuvius Ruhr, merge with Venus and Venetian Algae,

sell the Milky Way and subdivide the subsidi-
ary of submerged Atlantis; conglomerate the
Fifth dimension with the cleavage of the Fifth
Column; combine with Overkill and Under-
water testing, spike with Calcium Propionate
and advertise it subliminally in Vita-Mellon.
Flash: Hong Kong is up for grabs, you have
"Right of First Refusal" . . . Genghis Khan
(*Alone.*) Relief . . . release . . . I'm re-
laxed, at last. She's gone. My wife is dead.
Why did she have to die? Not for the reasons
the D.A. said in court. I didn't want to marry
my secretary. (Although she hoped for me.)
I didn't want to remove my wife only to replace her with another female. I needed living
space, I'm more than an appendage, I'm more
than part of a couple. She had to be removed.
I could no longer be a whole man. The more
I slept near her, the more we bathed in the
same tub, the more we ate from the same
plate, the more like her I became. Our clothes
were even in the same closet and drawers. It
drove me insane to look for my shirts among
her underpants. The children couldn't tell us
apart. There was only one thing to do. Kill
myself, or kill my female self. With her gone
my potency returned, my hair stopped falling
out, my muscles can push again against my
skin and leap from my bones when I walk.
With her gone, I've succeeded in pressing my
breasts back inside my chest where they be-
long. There is only one figure for my boys to

191

look up and see now. They're no longer confused and they'll grow into men, because now
they look up to find only one person. A man.
Me. Their father.

MICHAELS (*Goes back to his bed*): If they can see
through the bars, that is.

JASPERS: I won't be here long.

MICHAELS: You'll get out of here when they carry you
out to be laid beside your wife.

JASPERS: Never. Do you hear. Never. It's only me now.
Me and the boys. Since when did you get to
be such a smart mouth?

MICHAELS: Since I've been watching you all this time.
Boy, you really had me snowed. I thought you
knew the score about everything. But man,
your score is screwy. Big-shot shyster lawyer.
You were never gonna give me my share of
the cash. I don't think you even want it. I'm
not gonna kiss your ass any more, and I could
bash myself for having done it this long.

JASPERS: What's the matter, Michaels, you constipated?

MICHAELS: From you and your crumby schemes. That's
what. You think you're free but you're locked
up. How upside down can you get? Don't it
even bother you that she's dead? Don't it ever
get next to you in the night time? Don't it?
Don't it?

JASPERS: Never. I'm free of her. Never. This is what I
want.

MICHAELS: It will. You're spooked and you don't know it.

JASPERS (*Gets out of bed and goes to* GREGORY): I've changed my mind. I don't want you to sign this confession. Give it back.

GREGORY: Why? Why?

JASPERS: Would you like to get out of here?

GREGORY: I don't know.

JASPERS: What do you mean, you don't want to rot in here?

GREGORY: It's safe here. I can sleep here. I don't get into trouble here.

JASPERS: You've been in trouble the whole time here.

GREGORY: But not with cops, not with the judge, not with the jury.

JASPERS: You can get out. I've got money. I'll share.

GREGORY: I don't know.

JASPERS: I'll get you out, and I'll keep you out of trouble.

GREGORY: I don't know.

JASPERS: I'll take care of you. I know how. I have two boys of my own. You know my boys, I've told you about them.

GREGORY: Well . . . maybe . . . I could . . .

JASPERS: We'll make Michaels sign the confession that

he committed the murder, then dragged us in with him to save himself from the chair.

GREGORY: How can we do that? He's worked for you. He knows he worked for you. How can you convince him he did it?

JASPERS: The same way I convinced you. Come, I'll teach you how.

(JASPERS *mounts a pulpit*. GREGORY *and* MICHAELS *assume the position and posture of altar boys*.)

JASPERS (*A sermon: he builds this message to himself and his congregation to a high pitch of sublimity*): Dearly beloved . . . dearly, dearly dearly beloved. We are gathered here together to join hands in recognition. Dearly beloved, we are gathered here together to join minds for a purification. There is a man present. There is a man present. There is a man in our midst, a man accused. It is said this man desired the murder of his wife. His wife was murdered. Let us deliver him. He had been joined together with this wife in the bonds of holy matrimony. How could this man put asunder what God had joined? Let us join to deliver . . . let us join to devour the unhealthy choking fat of his guilt . . . Let us . . .

(*He looks at the congregation, clears his throat, tries to resume his former pitch, falters, and confronts himself*.)

Sometimes I have brief thoughts that God and I are wrong . . . I mean one. I mean one . . . one and the same. I don't mean wrong, I mean the opposite of wrong. What's happened to me?

(*He stops and tries to control himself. He listens.*)

Wait. Wait. I hear another heartbeat! Don't be afraid. You're always afraid to reach your hand to someone else for fear he'll light a fire to it!

(*He assumes a pose of ecclesiastical strength and resumes the pace and pitch of the opening section.*)

My message to you is—embrace! If you do not, if you do not learn to embrace then you will not be prepared to unlock. You will not know then, dearly beloved, you will not know then how to lose. Embrace! You will need all the strength from the ecstasy of that embrace in order to face what you will soon lose. You will lose. You will lose your mother. You will lose your father. You will lose your lover. Your eyes will dim. Your taste diffuse. Your gesture will cramp. Your judgment go askew. Your job will be usurped. Pleasure will fade; thought go in circles. You will lose your wife . . . she will be wrenched from the bosom of your attention. (*Thundering like a prophet*) You will lose your life. You will lose.

(*He is tired. He leans on the pulpit and talks very gently.*)

Let me offer my private parts as your first fruits. Dearly beloved, let us . . . Dearly beloved, let us . . . Dearly beloved, let us pray. . . . (*He collapses into the arms of* GREGORY *and* MICHAELS.)

MICHAELS (*As Richard, the eight-year-old*): Don't cry, Father.

GREGORY (*As Mark, the ten-year-old*): Don't cry, Father.

MICHAELS: Mommie's in heaven.

GREGORY: She's with God.

MICHAELS: Don't cry, Father.

GREGORY: Mommie's with God and she's smiling down on us.

JASPERS: Boys . . . my boys.

MICHAELS (*Gripping* JASPERS' *knees*): Please, please don't be sad, Daddy.

GREGORY (*Gripping* JASPERS' *shoulders*): Think of her smiling down on us all that way from heaven.

(*The two men lift* JASPERS *slowly and finally get him above their heads.*)

MICHAELS: You still have us.

GREGORY: You'll always have us, Dad. We'll never leave you. You're ours. We're yours. You're our father.

MICHAELS: Our father.

GREGORY: Our father . . . our Mother . . .

MICHAELS (*Chanting*): Thy Kingdom come . . .

GREGORY (*Chanting*): Come . . . the Kingdom . . .

MICHAELS (*Chanting*): Thy will be done.

GREGORY (*Chanting*): Hallowed be thy name. Name. Name. Name.

JASPERS (*Chanting*): Jaspers. Frank Jaspers.

MICHAELS (*Chanting*): On earth as it is in heaven.

JASPERS (*Chanting*): Frank Jaspers. Jaspers, Frank. Franklin Jaspers. Franklin Stowe Jaspers, Father.

MICHAEL (*Chanting*): We have you, Father.

GREGORY (*Chanting*): We hold you, Father.

TOGETHER (*Chanting*): Lean on us.

JASPERS (*Chanting*): Father, widower, murderer, my sons. Where are my sons? My sons. My fathers, my sons.

TOGETHER (*Chanting*): Our father. Our father. Our father. Our father. Lean on us.

(MICHAELS, *lowering* JASPERS' *legs, kisses* JASPERS' *knees.* GREGORY, *lowering* JASPERS' *shoulders, kisses* JASPERS' *temples.*)

JASPERS (*Chanting*): My sons.

197

MICHAELS *and* GREGORY (*Chanting*): Our Father. Ours.
(*The three men line up and face audience.
They lock arms and form a circle facing out-
ward. They move like a machine wheel.*)

JASPERS: Place labels on rubber roller.

TOGETHER: AND roller and roller and roller.

MICHAELS: Pull out the labels and feed . . .

GREGORY: . . . And feed into machine, gummed side
toward the roller.

TOGETHER: AND roller and roller and roller
AND rocker and rocker and rocker
AND roller and roller and roller
AND feeder and feeder and feeder
AND roller and roller and rocker!

JASPERS: This side

MICHAELS: Should face

GREGORY: You!

TOGETHER: And you and you and you and you and
you and you and you AND ROLLER AND
ROCKER. THIS SIDE SHOULD FACE
YOU. AND ROLLER AND ROCKER. (*The
wheel stops with* JASPERS *facing audience.*)

JASPERS: This side should face you!

CURTAIN

Keep Tightly Closed *has been produced by two important groups—the Open Theatre of New York, and the Firehouse Theatre of Minneapolis. Directors' notes for these productions follow.*

NOTES FOR THE
OPEN THEATRE PRODUCTION
By Peter Feldman

■

Keep Tightly Closed began as an actors' project of the Open Theatre. Three of them rehearsed it for about a month under the supervision of one of our actresses. The work stopped for the next month, because of a busy production schedule. At that point I was asked to direct the play, only two weeks and a few days before the scheduled opening, with one cast change necessary. The actors' morale was low because of the delays, the time limitations (some of us had daytime jobs and could only rehearse at night), the problems which had not been solved. The preliminary work they had done was very useful, but necessarily limited.

I began by having the actors work on improvisations for basic character and situation. These were of an abstract nature, dealing with dependency, enclosure, and isolation, and they threw the actors off guard. They did not expect me to put the script down so casually with two weeks to go before the opening; the shock jarred them into action. Before long we had established rapport both with each other (never difficult in our ensemble) and with what we were doing and could settle down to detailed work on the script.

Certain details of blocking were set quickly, because they expressed details of character relationships or set up a scene for actors to use as a springboard for further investigation and experimentation. An enormous amount of time then was spent trying, discarding, selecting. Since our actors work together so much in our workshops, and with our playwrights and directors, we can take many shortcuts with them based on previous experiences and a common frame of reference; moreover, there is little conflict between the actors' inventiveness and aims and the demands of the playwright. By the time *Keep Tightly Closed* opened, I could no longer tell where the inventiveness of the director left off and that of the actors had taken over, or where the script inspired us and where we enriched it.

Terry had enough confidence in me to allow me to cut portions of the script. [The acting (cut) version is the one printed here.] The pruning was done as we went along, sometimes at the suggestion of the actors, sometimes by me. The actors recognized the value of the play as an ensemble piece and so there was no resentment. In all, about three pages of dialogue were cut.

The production opened as scheduled.

The changes which take place all through *Keep Tightly Closed* are based on improvisations done in our workshops for the past three years. We call them transformations, although a friend has suggested the term "metamorphoses." The transformation is adapted from a Second City Workshop device but is not merely an acting stunt. It is an improvisation in which the established realities or "given circumstances" (the Method phrase) of the scene change several times during the course of the action. What may change are character and/or situation and/or time and/or objectives, etc. Whatever realities are established at the beginning are destroyed after a few minutes and replaced by others. Then these are in turn destroyed and replaced. These changes occur swiftly and *almost without transition,* until the audience's dependence upon any fixed reality is called into question. A member of our audience once said that these continual metamorphoses left him feeling "stationless," which is precisely the point.

Transformations, of course, have existed in film and theatre before in various forms. There is the vaudeville turn in which one character remains constant while the other goes through Jekyll and Hyde transformations, a variation on the famous "Slowly I turned" routine. There are Expressionistic plays such as Sorge's *The Beggar,* in which stylistic transformations are used to illuminate aspects of the central theme; but in that play each change is self-contained in its own scene. There are such pieces by Marceau as his *Birth, Youth, Old Age, and Death.*

In film, there are many examples of fantasy transformations, Fellini being only the most recent practitioner.

The transformation, besides questioning our notion of "reality" in a very graphic way, also raises certain questions about the nature of identity and the finitude of character. At the Open Theatre we tend to define character by what a person does that we can see, not by what society or his childhood experiences have produced in him. In this we have been influenced by many of the Absurdist playwrights, who have been redefining character since the end of World War II. In order to function in these plays the actor must build his characters in a new way, a fact which many Method teachers have not come to see. Stanislavski's last experiments were moving in this direction also: away from psychological motivation as a starting

201

point, toward the discovery of character through physical action, which becomes a symbol for metaphysical condition. It is a way to get beyond the nervous system into the soul.

We are not casual about character differentiation, but rely on the actor's choices and on his own personality to a great degree. Perhaps this is because we have questions about how much we all really exist; and we question whether subtle character differences really matter in the moment of facing up to the fact of our mortality in a godless world.

The machine-like scenes which open and close the play are also based on improvisations, although this sort of work with inanimate objects and external character adjustments, based on observation, would be familiar to any Method student. But again, we have taken this a little further in our work, using the machine impersonation as the basis of, or climax to, various scenes as a comment on the mechanical aspects of our life. The relationship of these machine impersonations to the lives of the three men in prison in the play is obvious enough. What is not so obvious, and what I would want to try to bring out when we revive the play this season, is that there is a certain sense in which the three men create their own jail cell and imprison themselves in it.

After the play opened, I had a talk with Gordon Rogoff in which he said that its most impressive aspect was the juxtaposition of naturalistic and non-naturalistic scenes. But I believe the play draws its peculiar tension from the relationship of all its elements, including one non-naturalistic scene next to another non-naturalistic one. Naturalism is not something that must be countered with non-naturalism; that is making naturalism more important than it is. The modes of behavior in this play all have equal value. Naturalism is just one of many styles, one of many worlds the play investigates.

Some of these worlds are clear from a reading of the script—naturalism, lots of tough-talking-prison-movie-ism, romantic

costume-drama-ism, vaudeville, pop, camp, semi-satirical dec-
lamation, automatism. Many of these were reinforced and re-
prised, and other forms were inserted right in the middle of
scenes. Many things we did were based on movies, and movie
characters or actors: Bogart, Newton, Widmark, Leo Gorcey,
a composite of Jack Hawkins and Sir C. Aubrey Smith; a kind
of composite of Everett Sloane in *The Lady From Shanghai*
and Edward G. Robinson in many roles and Sydney Green-
street in practically anything. There were places in which the
whole tone of the scene was lifted from movies, including
many moments from 1930's prison movies. The Custer-Indian
scene was a caricatured John Ford Western (with Kirk Doug-
las as White Fang); the scene beginning, "Tell me! You tell
me how you murdered my wife," was partly from trial movies
and partly from a trial improvisation we have done; the Captain John Smith scene was from costume epics, with just a
touch of Harry in the night.

Among the elements we reinforced or added were a dance
of pursuit and strangulation at the end of the scene between
the wife, the child, and Gregory; a shuffle-off-to-Buffalo into
a military march which ended in the bedmaking, just after the
vaudeville song and before the queen scene; a stylized,
pantomimed putting-on-of-the-vestments before the climactic
"Dearly Beloved" speech. The vaudeville song was choreographed by Peter Berry as a typical soft-shoe routine.

That we used dance and other movement so freely reflects
our interest in the physical expression of theatrical images. We
no longer feel that the spoken word is the dominant form of
theatre communication. To us, the visual image has become
just as pungent and poetic, especially in modern plays. The
actors have done a great deal of work in this area, and an
Open Theatre director knows that he can expect them to be
supple and inventive. The playwrights, too, use physical visual
images to enhance their plays.

What did we make of this wild, melodramatic play? A play about those who are tormented and those who torment; about imprisonment—literal, psychological and metaphysical; about dependency and fatherhood. No story, just a couple of incidents. Hardly any progression of character, in the conventional sense. I did take it that Jaspers' mind cracks completely at the end, and the "Dearly Beloved" speech shows him in the midst of a wild, pseudo-religious, ecstatic delusion: it was played broadly as a Cardinal Cushing oration.

It helped me think of the play as a kind of theatrical cubism. The author breaks up and reconstructs various facets of the same experience, thereby exposing all possible aspects of it. There is movement, disorientation, superimposition, refraction, new relations between events, a splintering of time and form. The play enlarges the scope of our transformations to say that the experiences and influences of our life must always be re-evaluated as modern events proliferate, and that none of these events is as it seems if you look at it from only one angle.

There is great irony in the juxtaposition of the melodrama to genuine isolation and torment. The pop and camp elements are typical of the new writing, iconoclastic and hard-edged. There is little tenderness in the play until those moments at the end between the sick father and his sons, which may be what the play is about, ultimately.

Comedy took its place as a most important force in this tortured play. The movie sequences, the vaudeville, the camped queen scene were all funny, often grotesque. There was very little subtlety.

With one or two exceptions (such as the Captain John Smith scene) the basic facts of the characterizations were revealed through all the transformations of the play: Gregory emerged as an amoral, high-strung, slightly demented and dangerous individual; Michaels as a lumpish tool, uncertain in his feelings about anything, vaguely disillusioned yet still held by his attraction to Jaspers; Jaspers as a cold and ruthless psychotic.

The play was performed on a rectangular platform, 16 x 13 feet, about three inches high, with the audience on two sides adjacent to each other. Off to one side, against the wall of the theatre, was a small three-step platform which was not used until the "Dearly Beloved" speech, when the actors crossed to it across a stretch of open floor and Jaspers mounted it as to a pulpit. Behind him was a lurid mural of a bloody woman, strangled and stabbed in her bathtub. The painting, by Esther Gilman, had certain real elements on it: a bloody stocking, hair from the woman's head, a mask for the face, the front page of a tabloid newspaper. Above Jaspers' head was a common, scoop-shaped light fixture from which hung a cheap, gaudy tassel.

In rehearsal, we found that a double-decker bunk bed was not necessary. I separated Jaspers' and Michaels' beds to opposite ends of the rehearsal loft with excellent results. Thereafter we used three cots in the upstage right corner of the large platform stage. Jaspers' cot was a couple of inches higher than the others'. It is fortunate that it worked out this way, as we could not afford to buy bunk beds anyway.

Most of the action took place on various parts of the large platform stage. But Gregory's speech about the trouble he had murdering Jaspers' wife was performed in the audience, going up the aisles. The military march was performed around the perimeter of the platform stage.

The men wore work clothes. The cots had army blankets. There were an ash tray, a cigarette, a piece of paper (the "confession"), a small note for Gregory to try to swallow. The lighting followed the mood and/or the playing areas. That was the extent of the physical production. Since the play goes into so many different worlds, it was necessary to avoid being too specific about the starting point: the sparsity of the physical production helped to keep the audience's attention on the actors and the shifting realities.

NOTES FOR THE
FIREHOUSE THEATRE PRODUCTION
By Sidney S. Walter

■

All of us are confined by certain limitations. As long as we expend our energy struggling against these limitations we are frustrated, impotent, hung-up. When we accept them we find freedom. It is not a matter of resignation to accept our limitations; it is a discovery of potential. Only within them can we realize joy and productivity. In *Keep Tightly Closed,* the jail cell is a metaphor for the prisons in which we are all confined.

Jail is the limitation which the three men in this play must accept, jail and each other. Jaspers cannot accept this. The play relates his journey from impossible, frustrating schemes for escape to an understanding that his fulfillment must be discovered within the context of imprisonment with the two other men.

Jaspers and Gregory are opposites. Jaspers is the planner, the hustler, the achiever. He is proud of his intellect and of his ability to dominate. Gregory is a sensualist. Jaspers is tormented until he can shed his pride and accept the inevitable with Gregory's simplicity and grace. Michaels is the middleman. In almost every transformation* Jaspers and Gregory relate through Michaels.

* Transformation is the term used by Joseph Chaikin to identify

206

The play is framed by the mechanical transformations, each one a stage in Jaspers' journey. In these the actors become part of a machine, interacting with each other and incorporating the dialogue into the workings of the machine. The first mechanical transformation is characterized by extreme tenseness, by jabbing and slapping motions. The second is patterned after the animated machines of TV commercials. It suggests the zany gaiety of the Bromo-Seltzer Kid. The characters are learning that they must cooperate, but their involvement is still superficial. In the last mechanical transformation we tried to inform the machine with human joy. The characters accept the limitations of their existence and satisfying relationships are possible. Jaspers accepts the other two as his sons; they accept him as their father. Having accepted, deeply satisfying relationships are possible.

Up to the re-enactment of the murder, the play is dominated by Gregory. His character is a startling combination of innocence and wickedness: in the author's words, "a piece of cake." He is a man without moral sensibilities, deriving a maximum of satisfaction from whatever situation circumstances force him into. The audience is alternately charmed and horrified by his excesses. This part of the play is gro-

---

an improvisational technique developed at the Open Theatre. I worked there for two years; Miss Terry is still working there. Transformation dramatizes those aspects of personality which in a naturalistic play would be implied by the sub-text. Transformations should not be thought of as dramatizations of fantasies but as exposures of those elements of personality which lie beneath the role which a human being assumes as his identity. We are aggregates of the most dramatic contradictions, but we try to present a consistent image. We are never completely successful in maintaining this image; in Miss Terry's plays the multiple roles beneath the identifying role burst through to reveal the complexities of relationships.

tesquely funny; its most vivid moments are those in which Gregory confronts the audience directly.

After the murder, Jaspers becomes the focal figure, and the play is much less funny. It reaches its climax when Jaspers confronts the audience as priest-evangelist. In the speech of loss we brought up the house lights and the actor playing Jaspers pointed to members of the audience as he described the loss which each of us must accept. The old Jaspers then dies in the funeral scene, borne on the shoulders of Gregory and Michaels. He is reborn in the last mechanical transformation as a character who has shed his pretensions and his pride and accepted his bonds to the other two men.

We did not attempt to make the scenes in which the three men play the roles which they have chosen to present to society much more real than the transformations into other roles. We took each scene as far as we could. We tried to make the Western scene as much like a John Wayne movie as we could; in the drag-queen scene the men became drag queens. In other words, we did not want to imply that Jaspers, Michaels, and Gregory were playing roles in the transformations—they transformed into different characters. In the priest scene the actor was not playing Jaspers playing a priest; he was simply playing a priest. The many transformations are not subsumed under the social personalities. Rather the characters are defined by all of the transformations, none of which should be considered as having more weight or significance than any other.

This presented an unusual acting problem. The play is really many short plays following one another without pause. The actor is not able to build a character slowly, but must plunge into each new role quickly and completely. It is generally assumed that good acting technique demands that an actor take time to prepare a character, but this is largely folklore. All three actors were able to encompass the abrupt and radical transitions with ease. It was one of the aspects of the show which they most enjoyed. It should be noted, however, that these three actors, like all actors cast in Firehouse productions, have the experience of meeting twice a week in a workshop devoted to developing new acting techniques. They have worked extensively on improvisational transformations.

We chose abrupt rather than gradual transitions because that seemed the most dramatic choice and the choice that the play demanded. Whenever possible, however, we tried to suggest the succeeding transformation in the final moment of the preceding one. In the vaudeville scene, for example, the routine ended with the three men in a somewhat effete pose, from which they became drag queens in the next scene.

Whenever possible we played lines and speeches to the audience. The event became a game that the actors and audience were playing together. Miss Terry devised many ingenious ways for the actors to confront the audience. We tried to exploit this writing technique by finding different attitudes for the actors to assume on each direct address. They teased, implored, and criticized. They embarrassed and they acknowledged embarrassment. They hid behind roles and they opened themselves completely.

In working on each scene we sought two keys: 1) What does the scene say about the relationships among the three men? 2) What is the style of the scene? Miss Terry uses popular art forms, especially movies, to make statements about her characters. When a well-known form was indicated we tried to present the scene in such a way that the audience would immediately recognize it. In the gangster scene, for example, we attempted to create the reality of a Hollywood movie about gangsters, not the reality of actual gangsters. The language of this scene is superbly right for creating a Hollywood style scene, entirely wrong for the creation of an actual gangster scene.

209

THE GLOAMING, OH MY DARLING

■

For My Grandmothers

PRODUCTION NOTES

■

There is no need for the actresses to be old. Any age will do. If the actresses cannot do a successful Irish accent, they should use whatever they are successful at. The accents of their mothers or grandmothers, or the accent of their native regions. No agony or time should be spent on the technical aspect of this—dwell on the relationships in the play—the relationships of the women to one another, to themselves, to their families, their country, to the past and future.

The scenery can be only two cots, or a nearly complete nursing-home room. If real hospital beds can be used, there is a way of cranking them so that Mr. Birdsong is completely hidden from the audience until he springs from the bed. This is fun, but it isn't necessary to the play.

The transitions should flow one into the other without pause or marking of any kind. The time slides in and out, and the final result should be that it is all the same time. The time can be compressed or extended, but it is all the same time. The intent is to see two lifetimes and certain aspects of the life of a country in one concentrated look.

The backbone of the play is the embrace of life, no matter how little of it is left.

THE GLOAMING,
OH MY DARLING

■

(*Two women sit on two chairs in a nursing home. There are two beds in the small sunny room. One of the beds is occupied, but the sheet and blanket are drawn up over the head of the occupant. The two old women speak in Irish accents.*)

MRS. TWEED: Ah yes, Mrs. Watermellon, and the days go by and the days go by and the days go by and the days go by, and by and by the days go by. My God, how the days go by!

MRS. WATERMELLON: From where I sit . . . I have to agree with you. But they don't go fast enough by, Mrs. Tweed, not by a half sight, not by a full sight. The world is waiting for the sunrise, and I'm the only one who knows where it begins.

MRS. TWEED: Why do you keep it a secret?

MRS. WATERMELLON: No secret. I've told everyone. I've told and told and told everyone.

MRS. TWEED: Where does it begin then?

MRS. WATERMELLON (*Slapping her breast*): Here. Right here. Right here it starts! From the old ticker it starts and pumps around and thumps around, coagulates in my belly and once a month bursts out onto the ground . . . but all the color's gone . . . all but one . . . all but . . . one. . .

MRS. TWEED: So that's where the sunrise went.

MRS. WATERMELLON: You three-minute egg. You runny, puny twelve week's old, three-minute egg. You're underdone and overripe. What do you know? You only learned to speak when you got mad enough . . . I'm going to sleep. I'd as soon live in the mud with the turtles as to have to converse with the likes of you.

MRS. TWEED: Don't talk like that. That hurts me.

MRS. WATERMELLON: Nothing can hurt you if your mind is on a high plain.

MRS. TWEED: If you go to sleep on me, then I'll let him go.

MRS. WATERMELLON: If you let him go, Mrs. Tweed, then I'll tell you where your daughter is.

MRS. TWEED: I won't listen.

MRS. WATERMELLON: Oh yes, you'll listen. You'll listen to me tell you where she is. It makes you cry and you hate to cry. But once you get started crying you wake up everyone, and then they'll give you an enema.

MRS. TWEED: I don't care if they do. There's nothing more to come out. They've tubed, and they've squirted, and they've radiated and they've intravened . . . There's nothing more to come out of me. I haven't had reason to pick my nose in two years.

MRS. WATERMELLON: Do you think he's awake yet?

MRS. TWEED: Mrs. Watermellon, what if someone comes to visit him?

MRS. WATERMELLON: I won't let them see him.

MRS. TWEED: You have to let them see him if they're his folks.

MRS. WATERMELLON: Nope, you dope, I don't.

MRS. TWEED: You do have to let folks see him. What else would folks be coming up here for, if not to see him.

MRS. WATERMELLON: Perhaps he's passed on—passed over. I'll say he's gone West. ANYWAY, Mrs. Tweed, he's mine now.

MRS. TWEED: Why, he's ours, Mrs. Watermellon. You can't have him all to yourself!

MRS. WATERMELLON: That's what I did in the night. I DIDN'T want you to find out, but since I see what a busybody you finally are, after all these bygone days, I'll tell you once and for all. He's mine!

MRS. TWEED: But we got him together. I carried the bottom end. You weak old tub, you couldn't even have lifted him from his bed by yourself. You'd have dropped and broken him. They'd have put us in jail for stealing and murder. They'd have electrocuted and hung us . . . they'd have . . .

MRS. WATERMELLON: Hush your mouth! Hush up. I won't have him disturbed by your temper.

MRS. TWEED: I'm going to give him back. Tonight I'll carry him back to the men's ward and tuck him in his crib.

MRS. WATERMELLON: No, you won't. He's mine.

MRS. TWEED: Ours.

MRS. WATERMELLON: Mine.

MRS. TWEED: Ours . . .

MRS. WATERMELLON: All right. All right, you pukey squashed robins egg, all right! All right, all right, you leftover maggot mangy mop rag. All right! All right, you dried-up, old snot rag, I'm going to tell you, I'M GOING TO TELL you right here and now. Do you hear me? I'm going to tell you right here and now.

MRS. TWEED: I don't want to hear. Not here. Not now.

VOICE (*A recorded voice of a young woman sings.*

WATERMELLON *and* TWEED *freeze in their places during the song*):

"In the gloaming, oh my darling,
When the lights are soft and low,
Will you think of me and love me
As you did once long ago?"

MRS. WATERMELLON (*Coming back to life*): I'm hungry for canned rhubarb! Never did get enough. My greedy little sister used to get up in the night when we's all asleep and sneak down to the fruit cellar and eat two quarts of rhubarb, every single night.

MRS. TWEED: She must a had the cleanest bowels in the whole country.

MRS. WATERMELLON: My mother had the best dinner. For her last birthday two days before she died my brother asked her what she wanted. She knew it was her last supper.

MRS. TWEED: Chicken baked in cream in the oven?

MRS. WATERMELLON: Nope, you dope. Pheasant she wanted. Cherrystone clams, six of them, roast pheasant and wild-blackberry pie. She ate every bit of it. We watched her. She ate it all up, every speck of it. Cherrystone clams, six of them, roast pheasant, and wild-blackberry pie. Licked her lips.

MRS. TWEED: That rings a bell. I had pheasant once. Pheasant under glass. Looked so pretty, I didn't eat it. Where was that?

MRS. WATERMELLON: You had it at the old Biltmore. She licked her lips and closed her eyes. She never opened them again.

MRS. TWEED: That rings a bell. Who'd I have it with? Did I taste it? Under a lovely glass bell. Who was I with?

MRS. WATERMELLON: You were with your husband, Mrs. Tweed. Your second husband. You did that on your anniversary. On your wedding anniversary, you dope. You've told me every one of your anniversary stories five hundred times a year.

MRS. TWEED (*Laughs*): It's gone from me. All gone from me. Fancy that, but it does ring a bell.

MRS. WATERMELLON: You can eat mushrooms under glass too. Don't you know?

MRS. TWEED: Myrtle Classen used to serve them at her bridge luncheons. Mushrooms, under glass. I didn't eat any of those either.

MRS. WATERMELLON: What have you done with him, Mrs. Tweed?

MRS. TWEED: I made him even.

MRS. WATERMELLON: WHAT have you done with him?

MRS. TWEED: What'll you give me if I tell, Mrs. Watermellon?

MRS. WATERMELLON: Tell.

MRS. TWEED: Give.

MRS. WATERMELLON: Tell.

MRS. TWEED: Give.

MRS. WATERMELLON: Tell, tell.

MRS. TWEED: Give, give.

MRS. WATERMELLON: Tell, tell, tell!

MRS. TWEED: Give, give, give!

MRS. WATERMELLON (*Melting*): I give.

MRS. TWEED: All up?

MRS. WATERMELLON: All.

MRS. TWEED: Say it. Say it all, Mrs. Watermellon.

MRS. WATERMELLON: I give it all up. I give it all up to
my uncle. My uncle. Uncle.

MRS. TWEED: Who is he? Who is he, your uncle, uncle?

MRS. WATERMELLON (*Exhausted*): You are. You . . .
are . . . Mrs. Tweed.

MRS TWEED: Then you've got to tell me what you did
to Mr. Birdsong in the night.

MRS. WATERMELLON: Now?

MRS. TWEED: Not a moment too late.

MRS. WATERMELLON: I . . . I married him. I married
Mr. Birdsong.

MRS. TWEED: No.

MRS. WATERMELLON: In the night, I lifted the covers

from his body and I married him. Mrs. Birdsong. Mrs.

MRS. TWEED: But he was ours. We brought him here
together.

MRS. WATERMELLON: In the night . . .

MRS. TWEED: It isn't fair. You didn't do it fair. He
was . . .

MRS. WATERMELLON: I didn't want to do it, because
we've been such good, such only friends. But
I didn't want to tell you 'cause I don't want
you to stop rubbing my back on rainy days.
I didn't want to tell you because I didn't want
you to stop cleaning my nails on Sunday morn-
ings. I didn't want to tell you because you eat
those hard-cooked carrots for me on Wednes-
day nights. I didn't want to tell you 'cause
you rub a nipple and make me feel sweet sixteen when we play boy friends. I didn't want
to tell you because you're all I've got . . .
you're all I've been given in this last twenty
years. You're all I've seen in this never-
never. I didn't want to tell you because you're
the only one who can see *me*. I didn't want to
tell you because you were all I had. But now
I've got Mr. Birdsong. Mr. and Mrs. Birdsong.

MRS. TWEED: Don't tell me that. You shouldn't have
told me that.

MRS. WATERMELLON: And you don't even know any
good lifetime stories. I've been shut up with

a life that never moved at all. The only thing you can remember is how . . .

MRS. TWEED: . . . Is how I rode out in the Maine snow night with my DOCTOR Father and he held his fur-coat arms around me on his horse and I sat in front of him with his fur-coat arms around me and I held his scratched and leather smelly doctor's bag. Held it tight so's not to drop it in the Maine snow night.

MRS. WATERMELLON: That's what I mean, just one sentimental perversion after another.

MRS. TWEED: There's nothing perverted about father love.

MRS. WATERMELLON: There is if there's something perverted about Father.

MRS. TWEED: Who?

MRS. WATERMELLON: You. You. You, Mrs. Tweed.

MRS. TWEED (*Trying to rise*): That did it. That did it. That just about did it in, all right.

MRS. WATERMELLON: Sit down, you old windbag.

MRS. TWEED: That did it. That did it, Mrs. Watermellon. That just about did it in, all right.

MRS. WATERMELLON: Sit down, you old battle-ax.

MRS. TWEED (*On a rising scale*): That did it. That did it. That just about did it. That did it all right.

MRS. WATERMELLON: Sit down, you old blister.

MRS. TWEED (*She bursts*): THAT DID IT! (*She explodes into a convulsive dance. She sings. As she sings her accent disappears*):

> That's done it, that's better.
> That's done it,
> What ease.
> That's done it,
> That's better.
> What took you so long,
> You tease?

MRS. WATERMELLON: Don't leave me. I forbid you to go. Don't leave me, Tweed. Come back. Don't leave me here alone with a man.

MRS. TWEED (*She dances herself down to the age of sixteen*): I'm so tired. I'm so tired and so done in. We drank and drank so much grape punch and then that gentle Keith Lewiston took me behind the schoolhouse and you know what he did?

MRS. WATERMELLON: He hitched you to his buggy and drove you round the yard.

MRS. TWEED (*Embracing her*): He soul kissed me. He kissed my soul. Like this.

MRS. WATERMELLON (*Dodges*): Don't start that mush again.

MRS. TWEED (*Still sixteen*): He kissed my soul. Like this. (*She plants a kiss finally on* MRS. WATER-MELLON'S *neck.*)

MRS. WATERMELLON (*She starts to howl in pain, but the howl changes to a kind of gargle and then to a girlish laugh. Her accent leaves also*): Did it make a strawberry? Did you make me a strawberry on my neck? (*Now* MRS. WATERMELLON *is also sixteen.*) Do it again and make a big red strawberry mark. Then we'll have to wear long scarves around our necks, to school, but everyone will know why. They'll think the boys kissed us behind the schoolhouse. Is it red yet? Is it strawberry red yet?

MRS. TWEED (*Coming back to old age, she knots an imaginary scarf around* MRS. WATERMELLON'S *neck and her Irish accent returns*): No—not —yet.

MRS. WATERMELLON (*Chokes and laughs as if strangling*): Don't. We're friends. We're best friends. We're girl friends. (*Her Irish accent returns.*) Don't kill me. I'm your mother.

MRS. TWEED: Save all that for Doctor. I'm on to you. Your smart-assed psycho—hology won't work on me any more. Save it for Mr. Birdsong. *If* you can find him.

MRS. WATERMELLON: What have you done with him?

MRS. TWEED: Wouldn't you like to know.

MRS. WATERMELLON: What have you done with him? What have you done with my . . .

MRS. TWEED: *Your* what?

225

MR. BIRDSONG (*He's still in a coma, but speaks out in a voice like W. C. Fields*): Stuck with the cattle through the storm. Dust blowed so hard couldn't see yer hand in front of yer face. Twister blowed us five hundred miles. Caught us in Illinois and set us down in Nebraska. Dust blowed bad, but I never lost a head nor did I even stop to make water.

MRS. WATERMELLON: I'm tired of trying to keep alive.

MRS. TWEED: We'll get off the shelf.

MRS. WATERMELLON: Canned beside the hybrid corn.

MRS. TWEED: And the pickles.

MRS. WATERMELLON: And the piccalilli.

MRS. TWEED: And the bread and butters.

MRS. WATERMELLON: Apple butter.

MRS. TWEED: Watermelon relish.

MR. BIRDSONG: We kept right on putting our lives on the line because some fool gave the order.

MRS. WATERMELLON: Found a family. All I wanted was to found a great family.

MRS. TWEED: I worked hard. The wire factory gave me a good pension. I could still run up and down ladders as good as the men.

MR. BIRDSONG: The heathens want ours. They've infiltrated us in plain clothes. The heathen emissaries of Satan want to sabotage us. Scorch that earth, boys. That's the ticket. I want to get back to my bride.

MRS. TWEED: No one cares what we do now, Mrs. Watermellon, we can share him. We can both be Mrs. Birdsongs. The Mormons done it and God didn't get mad at them.

MRS. WATERMELLON: In the night I climbed into his bed and married him.

MRS. TWEED (*Begins to cry very quietly*): No. No. No. I can't believe it. You promised we'd share him. And to think I trusted you. And to think I loved you like a dear sister. And to think I gave you all my tender feelings for all these whitehouse years. AND TO THINK . . . and to . . .

MRS. WATERMELLON: Stop that yipping. It's your own fault. You left me all alone in the night. You went to sleep. You didn't keep watch. You turned out the light and went to sleep. They'd have shot you for that in World War I. You stopped guarding. I had to marry someone. I can't die childless. I refuse!

MRS. TWEED: Impossible! You have eleven children living, forty-nine grandchildren living, twenty great grandchildren living and three on the way. There's a lot of biscuit in your oven, and your ovens' ovens.

MRS. WATERMELLON: I just wanted to make it even with you. You had two husbands, you, you white and wizened shrimp. Two husbands! You knew two cocks of the walk in your time. Why should I take a back seat? Why should you know more than me?

MRS. TWEED: Is that your fountain of knowledge? I'll never get over this. Never, never. After all the friends we've been through. I'm going to divorce you.

MRS. WATERMELLON: I don't care. I'm a newlywed. I have security.

MRS. TWEED: I'll say! There's nothing more secure than a coma. HE'S BEEN IN THAT COMA FOR EIGHTY DAYS.

MRS. WATERMELLON: It'll make our adjustment easier.

MRS. TWEED: Adjustment?

MRS. WATERMELLON (*Inordinately satisfied*): To married life. Since only one of us has to change his ways, we should become compatible twice as fast.

MRS. TWEED (*Very formal*): Mrs. Watermellon, I'm going to ring for the nurse to change my room.

MRS. WATERMELLON (*Equally formal*): Mrs. Tweed, you better ring for the nurse to change your pants. See there, you've messed again.

MRS. TWEED: You're fooling me.

MRS. WATERMELLON: Maybe I am fooling you, but Mother Nature isn't. Ring for the nurse. Ring,

ring, ring, ring, ring, ring. Tick a lock, this
is a magic spot.

MRS. TWEED: Don't be mad to me any more.

MRS. WATERMELLON: Tick a lock, this is a magic spot.

MRS. TWEED: Don't be mad to me any more.

MR. BIRDSONG: Everywhere you look there's busloads
of foreigners. Rats are infiltrating our ranks.

MRS. TWEED: I hear a man's voice. Listen. Did you hear
it?

MRS. WATERMELLON: It's your longing. Your longing
rising up and talking to you.

MRS. TWEED: Sounds like my granddad. Just like him
when he come back from the war.

MRS. WATERMELLON: I don't hear anything but your
heart ticks getting fainter and fainter.

MRS. TWEED: Don't be so nice to me. You know I'm
going to die, that's why you're so nice to me.

MRS. WATERMELLON: Nonsense. You're not leaving before me. You're not leaving me alone in this
hotel.

MR. BIRDSONG (MRS. TWEED *and* MRS. WATERMELLON
don't react to MR. BIRDSONG *when he rises
from bed.* BIRDSONG *rises from his bed and
stalks around the room, mounts a box to
harangue the crowd—his voice now sounds
like Teddy Roosevelt*): As U.S. veteran of

229

the Indian Wars, I've come here before you to alarm you. Sons of Liberty unite. Smash the rats of the world. We must cut off their bloody hands. They're bringing this land that I love to wreck and ruin. Wreck and ruin to our God-given America. Murderers of women and children, red rats making balcony speeches. Balcony speeches by the feeble-minded mockers of God. That's the stink of Satan, boys. The stink of the murderers of Americans. The stink smelled is the stink from Satan. Satan who uses the body as a house to live in. The stink of Satan once smelled coming from these bodies is never forgotten. They want to make the United States and Mexico and Canada and Alaska into a death trap. Declare war on these stinking infiltrators. They've made it easy to burn up American bodies in the fiery furnaces of every hospital and prison. American Veterans of foreign wars, boys. Unite to fight. Unite to fight before they drug every one of us with their poisoned needles. Every man has been sexually destroyed by the needle while asleep. Fight the needle, boys. Don't let them burn up our unborn children. Why was Roosevelt murdered? Why was Kennedy murdered? Why was Stevenson murdered? The rat bonecrushers of the world are out to get us, all us American Veterans captive in these hospital jails. Unite to fight the rats, boys. Unite to fight the rats. (*He returns to his bed and his coma.*)

VOICE (*The woman's voice is heard again*):

> "In the gloaming, oh my darling,
> When the lights are soft and low,
> Will you think of me and love me
> As you did once long ago?"

MRS. WATERMELLON: I love President Kennedy.

MRS. TWEED: Makes you feel good just to look at him.

NURSE (*Enters with a fixed smile.* MRS. TWEED *and* MRS. WATERMELLON *rush to hide the man. They both get on the bed and spread their nightgowns over him. They lapse into their oldest age*): All right, you two—smarten up and look alive. (*She manhandles them—pushing and pulling them into some sort of erect state. They fall back to position like rag dolls —half cackling and half gurgling.*) I said look alive! You're going to have a visit. Your families have come to pay their monthly respects. Look alive, I said, or they'll think we're not taking good care of you.

MRS. WATERMELLON (*Frightened of the* NURSE): This woman's molesting me.

NURSE: Hold your head up so I can get some rouge on that pasty cheek.

MRS. WATERMELLON: This woman is molesting me.

NURSE: Hold still, you old hag. I got to get some life in your face.

MRS. WATERMELLON: I'll tell Dr. Sam on you and Dr. Ben and Dr. Jim, too, and God and everybody.

NURSE (*To* MRS. TWEED): Your turn now, you little old crab.

MRS. TWEED (*Playfully*): What'll you give me if I let ya?

NURSE: Dirty-minded old ladies. If your family could only hear you.

MR. BIRDSONG (*Under the ladies, belches*): I rode five hundred miles with my cattle in the dust storm and never stopped once to make water. (WATERMELLON *mouths the lines.*)

NURSE: Who said that?

MRS. TWEED: She did—she always brags about how strong she used to be.

NURSE: Show me a little strength now. Sit up and look out of your eyes.

(MRS. TWEED *bites the nurse; the* NURSE *slaps* TWEED.)

NURSE: Now there's some real color in your cheeks.

MRS. WATERMELLON (*Howls*): This woman is molesting us! (*The family enters.*)

NURSE (*Like an overly cheerful demented Katherine Hepburn*): We're feeling very well today. We're glad to see our family today. (*She exits.*) Our family is glad to see us today.

SON WATERMELLON (*Accompanied by his* SON *and* DAUGHTER): Mother! (*He goes to her, ultra-beaming.*) You look wonderful! Doesn't she look wonderful, kids?

SON *and* DAUGHTER (*Flatly*): You look wonderful. You look wonderful. Grandma, you look wonderful.

MRS. WATERMELLON: Who's there? Is there anyone there? Knock once for yes.

DAUGHTER TWEED (*Accompanied by her* SON *and* DAUGHTER, *crosses to* MRS. TWEED): Oh, Mother, you look wonderful. Doesn't she look just wonderful kids? Tell Mother how wonderful she looks.

SON *and* DAUGHTER (*Run at* TWEED): You look wonderful, Grandma—you look just wonderful. (*They climb all over her.*)

MRS. TWEED (*Nearly suffocating*): My dear children —my pretty grandchildren. Grandma loves you so much.

DAUGHTER TWEED (*As children swarm all over* TWEED, *kissing and pummeling her*): They love you so much, Mother. Isn't it wonderful for them that you're still alive?

GRANDSON *and* GRANDDAUGHTER TWEED: You feel just wonderful, Grandmother—just wonderful. (*They kiss and hug* TWEED *while she chokes and gasps.*)

233

SON WATERMELLON: Just sign right here, Mother. Here. I'll hold your hand around the pen.

MRS. WATERMELLON: What is it? Who are you?

SON WATERMELLON: I'm so grateful you haven't lost your sense of humor. Mother, you look downright beautiful. Color in your cheeks and everything. This isn't such a bad place after all, is it?

MRS. WATERMELLON (*Knocks once for yes*): You look a bit familiar around the eyes. I kept company with a young man once had shifty eyes kinda like yours.

SON WATERMELLON (*Laughs heartily*): Did you hear that, kids?

KIDS (*Flat and bored*): Hear what, Father?

SON WATERMELLON: Same old doll. What a doll my dear old mother was and still is. Just like the gal that married dear old Dad.

KIDS (*Flat*): Dear old shifty-eyed Dad.

SON WATERMELLON: Thanks for signing, honey-love. Makes it a lot easier for me now. Now look, sweetheart—you won't be seeing us for three months or so. Marge and the kids and I are going to Europe, but we'll send you a present from every port. How's about that? Give us a big smile and a kiss goodbye.

MRS. WATERMELLON: Then will you go?

SON WATERMELLON (*Hurt*): Mother! I had to take a day off from work and the kids out of school to drive up here! Marge is stuck with booking the passage.

MRS. WATERMELLON (*Turns off—sighs—lies back down*): I'll be all right. Don't worry about me.

SON WATERMELLON: Mother, don't be like this.

MRS. WATERMELLON: Don't worry, son, I won't *be* for much longer.

SON WATERMELLON (*Kisses her on cheek*): Goodbye, old girl.

KIDS: Goodbye, old girl. (*They exit.*)

MRS. WATERMELLON: Is there anyone there?

MRS. TWEED (*To* DAUGHTER): Dorothy, where's your sister, Laura?

DAUGHTER TWEED: She isn't well, Mother. She has a bad cold. She was afraid she'd give it to you —and with your condition you know it could develop into pneumonia and you know . . . (*She makes an explosive gesture.*)

MRS. TWEED: Well, tell her I thank her for her consideration but I'd like to see her face once in a while.

DAUGHTER TWEED: Well, Mother, we got to be getting back, I guess—got the dogs and cats to feed.

KIDS: They sure do get mad at us if they don't get their dinner on time.

DAUGHTER TWEED: It sure was just wonderful to see you and see how good you look and how happy you look. That old lady who shares the room with you looks quiet and nice, too.

MRS. TWEED: Dorothy—take me home.

DAUGHTER TWEED: You know I'd love to, but you know what I'm up against with Harry.

MRS. TWEED: Dorothy, your children tire me.

DAUGHTER TWEED (*Freezing up*): Goodbye, Mother. I'll see you next month. I thought you'd want to see your own grandchildren.

MRS. TWEED: I've seen enough.

DAUGHTER TWEED (*Gathering her children and leaving in a hurt rage*): The sun always rose and set on Laura's head and it still does. And she hasn't been to see you in fifty years.

MRS. WATERMELLON: Is there anyone here?

MRS. TWEED: No, thank God. They've gone.

MRS. WATERMELLON: They didn't take him?

MRS. TWEED: I stopped them from it. I told them he'd eloped with a local tramp.

MRS. WATERMELLON: Where is he now?

MRS. TWEED: Under you, you old tub. I hope you haven't smothered him to death.

MRS. WATERMELLON (*Feeling* MR. BIRDSONG): Here's his head. (*She puts her ear to his chest.*) I hear a beat. Far away—a sweet little beat. (*She lifts the sheet and counts his arms.*) One, two. (*Counts his legs.*) One, two. (*Counts his sex.*) One, two, three. I'm glad it has a handle on it. My husband said he wouldn't accept the baby otherwise.

MRS. TWEED: Let me see his tiny hands. Oh, oh, the fingernails! (*She kisses the fingernails of* MR. BIRDSONG.)

MRS. WATERMELLON: Why are you crying? A new baby should fill you with joy. Joy!

MRS. TWEED: These fingernails. Look how tiny, the size of a pin head! And sharp! Oh, oh, the fingernails.

MRS. WATERMELLON: God love him. A new life. God love it, God love it, God love it! (*She cuddles* MR. BIRDSONG.)

MRS. TWEED: God spelled backwards is dog.

MRS. WATERMELLON: A son, a son, we have a son. A son from God. (MR. BIRDSONG *gurgles like an infant.*)

MRS. TWEED: Watch out for the teeth. They grow fast. My left nipple still carries a scar.

MR. BIRDSONG: It was scorch the earth . . . scorch the earth of every village we took. After Lieutenant Pike found his brother scalped and his

guts strewn across the plain for the wolves to
munch, we were ordered to cut down every
peach tree, fill every irrigation ditch—burn
every lodge and kill every horse, woman, and
child of the Navaho.

MRS. WATERMELLON: He'll make his mother proud.

MRS. TWEED: My turn. (*She takes hold of* MR. BIRD-
SONG. MRS. WATERMELLON *holds on and
glares.*) You act as if you did it all yourself.

MRS. WATERMELLON: I did. It was my idea.

MRS. TWEED: Not even you and forty million prayers
could have raised him.

MRS. WATERMELLON: It was my idea. All you were was
a pair of arms.

MRS. TWEED: And a good strong back—which you lack.

MR. BIRDSONG (*A young officer returning to Illinois on
leave*): Mother! (*To* MRS. WATERMELLON)
It's fine to be home.

MRS. WATERMELLON: You're thin.

MR. BIRDSONG: Not for long. (*To* TWEED) And what
have we here—grown up and pretty as a
prairie flower.

MRS. TWEED (*Shyly*): I can still whip you on a fair day,
Elijah.

MR. BIRDSONG (*Advancing confidently and taking her
wrists*): 'Tis fair today, Susan.

MRS. TWEED (*Wilts and nearly swoons*): Mrs. Watermellon, your son's forgot his manners!

MRS. WATERMELLON: Lige! Leave go that gal or marry her.

MR. BIRDSONG (*To* TWEED): I stayed with our cattle from here to Nebraska. It was the mightiest dust storm with twisters any man could remember. I rode five hundred miles without stopping to make water. I didn't lose a head. Marry me.

MRS. TWEED: Marry me. Marry me. (*She goes into a slow-motion waltz with* BIRDSONG—MRS. WATERMELLON *joins them—while the voice of a woman sings a verse of "In the Gloaming."*)

MR. BIRDSONG (*They are at a picnic on the grass*): I have my orders, gals—ship out tomorrow. I'll miss your pretty faces—let's have one last roll.

MRS. TWEED *and* MRS. WATERMELLON: You can't go, Donny—you've only been with us a week.

MR. BIRDSONG: Case you didn't hear it, babes, there's a war on. I killed off more than my quota of Huns and now good Old Uncle's sending me against the slants. What a secret weapon to throw at the Japs.

MRS. TWEED *and* MRS. WATERMELLON (*Leap on him and roll him around in the grass, kissing and stroking him*): The lucky Japs. The lucky Japs. You come back to us, you big, big stud. You hear, you come back to us.

MR. BIRDSONG: I rode all night, couldn't see a thing but I heard 'em. The dust so thick I couldn't make out the body of a single cow—but I felt 'em—five hundred miles into the twister and I never lost a head nor did I even stop to make water.

MRS. TWEED: I go out of my mind over a man in uniform.

MRS. WATERMELLON: I go into my mind with a man in my bed. (*She gets* MR. BIRDSONG *back to bed.*)

MRS. TWEED: They'll catch you.

MRS. WATERMELLON: If they catch me—they'll have you too.

MR. BIRDSONG (*As he's being put to bed*): The Navaho all got up in their peaked plumed leather caps, blankets draped and heads held high—looked like a battalion of Roman Legionnaires. I felt time had slipped and slided and folded over—there I am in New Mexico fighting Roman warriors.

MRS. WATERMELLON: I can see the sunset, can you?

MRS. TWEED: Filters through.

MRS. WATERMELLON: The older I get the hotter I like it.

MRS. TWEED: You'll love it down below.

MRS. WATERMELLON: I'll turn you in. I'll tell the doctor.

MRS. TWEED: What could you tell the doctor?

MRS. WATERMELLON: How you follow him through the hall. How you don't have any pain in your chest and neck. You just crybaby about it so that he'll lift your nightgown and listen to your heartbeat through your dried-up titties.

MRS. TWEED: Yes, it's true. I like that.

MRS. WATERMELLON: No decency.

MRS. TWEED: Nonsense.

MRS. WATERMELLON: Of all the billions of Chinese in the world I have to be incarcerated with you. I served my time in the family way, I earned my arms and legs, I could drive from one town to another and visit New York. You'd think I'd have the right to choose my own cellmate, but no, no, I was placed in a place, it was planned and weighed, and examined, and organized for me. It was arranged. You were arranged for my best interests. I'd kill myself if they'd give me a sharp instrument.

MRS. TWEED: Your tongue will do.

MRS. WATERMELLON: Living with me has done you some improvement.

MRS. TWEED: You could do worse. You could be with balmy Mary McLemon. She spends every day picking nits off her clothes and her roommates. How'd you like her monkey hands and eyes all over you twenty-four hours a day. Or

whining Mary McOrange who complains if
it's hot and complains if it's cold and complains if the sun comes up and complains if it
don't and complains if she's dry and complains
if she's wet and complains if she lives and
complains if she dies.

MRS. WATERMELLON: Maybe I am fooling you, but old
Mother isn't. Tick a lock, this is a magic spot.

MRS. TWEED: Don't be bad to me any more.

MRS. WATERMELLON: Maybe I am fooling you.

MRS. TWEED: Don't be mean to me any more.

MRS. WATERMELLON: Maybe I am fooling you, but I'm
not responsible. No, I'm not—not any—any
more. I'm not.

MRS. TWEED: I'm going to call your mother. I'll fly her
here on a plane and have you committed. I'm
going to phone your son. I'm going to fly him
here and have you committed. I am. I will.
You'll be committed.

MRS. WATERMELLON: Dry up, you old fart. I already
am.

NURSE (*Entering with tray*): Time for cream of wheat.
(*She smiles as she says this, but her voice
is flat and mechanical.* TWEED *and* WATER-
MELLON *dive for their beds to hide* BIRDSONG
again.) Time for your creamy wheat. Time
for your wheat. Your cream's all gone. Time
for the heap, the wheat's all dry. Sit up like

good wrinkled girls and dribble it down your chins. Time for your cream of wheat, the sugar's all gone.

𝔐RS. WATERMELLON: I'm tired of being a middleman for that pap. Flush it down the nearest john!

𝔑URSE: I'll eat it myself. I'll eat it all up.

MRS. TWEED: It's worms. Look at her eat the pail full of worms.

MRS. WATERMELLON: You got it all wrong, Tweed. That's the worm and she's eating herself.

MRS. TWEED: Herself. And so she is. And to think of that.

MRS. WATERMELLON (*Laughing and slapping* MRS. TWEED *on a knee*): It's rich and richer and so so rich. I'd not thought it possible, but she's beaten us to it.

MRS. TWEED: Beaten us to it.

MRS. WATERMELLON: Yes, she's beaten us to it. Who'd ever have thought that she'd be the first worm. And she's done it before us.

MRS. TWEED: And we're so much older.

MRS. WATERMELLON: Of course we are. Nobody here could dare to be as old as we are. And look at that. Will you just look at that white worm. She's had the audacity to be a worm before us.

MRS. TWEED: And we're so much older.

NURSE: Time for your heat, the salve's all spread. Time for your bed, the sheet's all red. Time for the heap, the wheat's all cooked. Time for the deep, the syringe is plunged.

MRS. WATERMELLON *and* MRS. TWEED: And we're so much older. Nobody would dare to be as old or older. And we're so much older. (*They hold on to one another.*)

MRS. WATERMELLON: And older.

MRS. TWEED: And older.

MRS. WATERMELLON: In order.

MRS. TWEED: And older.

MRS. WATERMELLON: Tonight we'll be older still.

MRS. TWEED: In order.

MRS. WATERMELLON: If you'll stay up with me all night, then I'll let you.

NURSE: Time for the . . .

MRS. WATERMELLON: Keep right on eating and don't interrupt me.

NURSE: Time for the deep, the syringe is plunged. (*She gives them each a shot.*)

MRS. TWEED (*Taking* MRS. WATERMELLON'S *hand*): I won't close an eye.

MRS. WATERMELLON: Swear?

MRS. TWEED: I swear by Almighty God and little Lord Jesus asleep in the hay.

MRS. WATERMELLON: Then I'll take you back.

MRS. TWEED: Do you promise?

MRS. WATERMELLON: I promise.

MRS. TWEED: Is he ours?

MRS. WATERMELLON: Since we're older together in order, then I do believe that we can now share him.

MRS. TWEED: Then I'll take *you* back. The two Mrs. Birdsongs!

NURSE: Time for your milk, the white's at night. Time for the drink to put you in the pink. Time for the chalk, you're in the drink.

MRS. WATERMELLON (*To the* NURSE): Will you get out of here? Can't you see you're interfering with a honeymoon?

NURSE (*Smiling, leaves*): Only a few more to pin, then back to my bin. Time for a sleep, the light's turned out. Time for the deep, the syringe is shoved. (*She's gone.*)

MRS. WATERMELLON *and* MRS. TWEED (*They turn to one another*): How *do* you do, Mrs. Birdsong? How do *you* do, Mrs. Birdsong? (*They begin to laugh and burst out of their age. The Irish accents disappear also.*)

THAT DID IT. THAT DID IT. THANK GOD, THAT DID IT.

(*They jump like young women, leap, float,*

*bump into each other with gaiety, sing and
end in a tumble on the floor.*)

THAT did it, that's better.
That's done it,
What ease.
That did it, that's done it,
That's better.
What took you so long,
What took you so long,
Whatever on earth took you so long?

VOICES (*Two women sing very slowly in harmony
while* MRS. TWEED *and* MRS. WATERMELLON
freeze):

"In the gloaming, oh my darling,
When the lights are soft and low,
Will you think of me and love me
As you did once long ago?"

MRS. TWEED *and* MRS. WATERMELLON:
YOU TEASE
YOU TEASE
YOU TEASE
WHAT TOOK YOU SO LONG?

(*They jump up fiercely on the last line, still
laughing. But now they change to a blank
stare and say the final line in a singsong—
death has grabbed them by the back of the
neck*):

WHAT TOOK YOU SO LONG? SO LONG!
SO LONG! SO LONG?

(Then happily, saying goodbye—their arms around each other—they look out at the audience and smile):

SO LONG . . .

CURTAIN

Music for

VIET ROCK

and

COMINGS AND GOINGS

■

by
Marianne de Pury

VIET ROCK

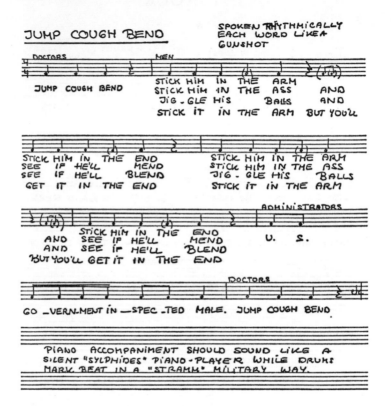

JUMP COUGH BEND

SPOKEN RHYTHMICALLY
EACH WORD LIKE A
GUNSHOT

PIANO ACCOMPANIMENT SHOULD SOUND LIKE A
SILENT "SYLPHIDES" PIANO-PLAYER WHILE DRUMS
MARK BEAT IN A "STRAMM" MILITARY WAY.

GOODBYE MY GOOD BOY

NOW THAT YOU ARE UP SO TALL I
HAVE TO SHARE YOU WITH THE WORLD BUT I CAN'T BE NICE ALL THE
TIME I GET MAD AND UP COMES MY GALL GOOD
BYE MY GOOD BOY GOOD BYE MY GOOD BOY GO QUICK

WAR AU GOGO

WELCOME TO SHANGRI-LA

To be spoken or sung verr very high, falsetto-like
Accompaniment should include Eastern percussions
such as woodblock, bamboo hangers, gongs etc.

TO THE JUNGLE MARCH

SNARE DRUM - POSSIBLY TRUMPET ACCOMPANIMENT.

"STRAMM"

TO THE JUNGLE MARCH THROUGH THE JUNGLE GORE

TO THE JUNGLE MARCH THROUGH THE JUNGLE ROAR WE'RE

OFF TO FIGHT FOR VIET. NAM WE WILL DIS - PLAY OUR

MIGHT WE'RE OFF TO WIN FOR VIET NAM WE'RE FIGHTING FOR

PLEASE GOD

MEN DIE YOUNG   (BITTER)

CARE-FUL WHAT YOU CHOOSE OR YOU'LL BE A-LONE THE

NEXT TWENTY YEARS BE-CAUSE MEN DIE YOUNG MY DEAR BE

CAUSE MEN DIE YOUNG YOU DON'T WANT TO

LOSE THE CHANCE TO CO-VER YOUR BETS SO

274

GOOTCH LET'S GET TO SAIGON AND BLITZ THE BARS WE'LL

LOAD UP ON BOOZE TILL WE SEE STARS TILL WE SEE STARS IN HER

HOOTCHIE COOTCH AND LOVE ALL NIGHT TO THE GOONIE GOOTCH TILL WE SEE

STARS TILL WE SEE STARS TILL WE SEE STARS TILL WE SEE STARS

CLOSE YOUR EYES

COMINGS AND GOINGS

■

COMINGS AND GOINGS

sung lightly, as in jest.

IN..SIDE OUT..SIDE ALL A-ROUND UP.SIDE DOWN TUR.NING GLI.DING

IN..SIDE OUT..SIDE RIGHT A.LONG GALLO..PING JUMP CATCH ME SWEET

SPOKEN

HARD HOLD ON TIGHT UPSADAISY IN..SIDE OUT..SIDE SHALL WE

SPOKEN

GO IN? RIGHT A..WAY IN..SIDE IN!

(HE) HA..VEN'T J MET YOU SOMEWHERE BE___FORE? ON THE

STEPS OF EL_SI___NORE? AT THE FILM OF E_LEA_

NOR? JUST IN ___SIDE THE BAR.BARY SHORE?

(SHE) NO NO NO J DON'T THINK SO AL___THOUGH J'D LIKE TO SLIP WITH YOU BE—

HIND THE DOOR (HE) WHAT MORE WHAT MORE WHAT MORE COULD ANY

MAN ASK OF A NEW MAID? (SHE) THEN SHALL WE SLIP

THEN SHALL WE DIP IN—TO A LOVE TIME TRAVEL TO A

HOT CLIME (HE) WHAT MORE WHAT MORE WHAT MORE COULD A·NY MAN

ASK OF A NEW MAID?

(TOGETHER) THEN WE'LL DIP WE'LL SLIP WE'LL GLIDE WE'LL HIDE WE'LL

SLIDE IN—TO LOVE TIME IN--TO LOVE TIME IN-

TO LOVE TIME THEN WE'LL DIP WE'LL SLIP WE'LL GLIDE WE'LL

HIDE WE'LL SLIDE IN—TO LOVE TIME IN—TO

LOVE TIME IN—TO LOVE TIME IN——TO LOVE TIME

LOVE TIME LOVE TIME LOVE TIME LOVE TIME